T0194661

An Analysis of

Zora Neale Hurston's

"Characteristics of Negro Expression"

Mercedes Aguirre
with
Benjamin R. Lempert

Published by Macat International Ltd
24:13 Coda Centre, 189 Munster Road, London SW6 6AW.

Distributed exclusively by Routledge
2 Park Square, Milton Park, Abingdon, Oxon OX14 4RN
711 Third Avenue, New York, NY 10017, USA

Routledge is an imprint of the Taylor & Francis Group, an informa business

www.macat.com
info@macat.com

Cataloguing in Publication Data
A catalogue record for this book is available from the British Library.
Library of Congress Cataloguing-in-Publication Data is available upon request.
Cover illustration: Kim Thompson

ISBN 978-1-912302-87-1 (hardback)
ISBN 978-1-912128-11-2 (paperback)
ISBN 978-1-912281-75-6 (e-book)

Notice
The information in this book is designed to orientate readers of the work under analysis,
to elucidate and contextualise its key ideas and themes, and to aid in the development
of critical thinking skills. It is not meant to be used, nor should it be used, as a
substitute for original thinking or in place of original writing or research. References and
notes are provided for informational purposes and their presence does not constitute
endorsement of the information or opinions therein. This book is presented solely for
educational purposes. It is sold on the understanding that the publisher is not engaged
to provide any scholarly advice. The publisher has made every effort to ensure that
this book is accurate and up-to-date, but makes no warranties or representations with
regard to the completeness or reliability of the information it contains. The information
and the opinions provided herein are not guaranteed or warranted to produce particular
results and may not be suitable for students of every ability. The publisher shall not be
liable for any loss, damage or disruption arising from any errors or omissions, or from
the use of this book, including, but not limited to, special, incidental, consequential or
other damages caused, or alleged to have been caused, directly or indirectly, by the
information contained within.

CONTENTS

THE MACAT LIBRARY

The Macat Library is a series of unique academic explorations of seminal works in the humanities and social sciences – books and papers that have had a significant and widely recognised impact on their disciplines. It has been created to serve as much more than just a summary of what lies between the covers of a great book. It illuminates and explores the influences on, ideas of, and impact of that book. Our goal is to offer a learning resource that encourages critical thinking and fosters a better, deeper understanding of important ideas.

Each publication is divided into three Sections: Influences, Ideas, and Impact. Each Section has four Modules. These explore every important facet of the work, and the responses to it.

This Section-Module structure makes a Macat Library book easy to use, but it has another important feature. Because each Macat book is written to the same format, it is possible (and encouraged!) to cross-reference multiple Macat books along the same lines of inquiry or research. This allows the reader to open up interesting interdisciplinary pathways.

To further aid your reading, lists of glossary terms and people mentioned are included at the end of this book (these are indicated by an asterisk [*] throughout) – as well as a list of works cited.

Macat has worked with the University of Cambridge to identify the elements of critical thinking and understand the ways in which six different skills combine to enable effective thinking.
Three allow us to fully understand a problem; three more give us the tools to solve it. Together, these six skills make up the **PACIER** model of critical thinking. They are:

ANALYSIS – understanding how an argument is built
EVALUATION – exploring the strengths and weaknesses of an argument
INTERPRETATION – understanding issues of meaning

CREATIVE THINKING – coming up with new ideas and fresh connections
PROBLEM-SOLVING – producing strong solutions
REASONING – creating strong arguments

To find out more, visit **WWW.MACAT.COM.**

CRITICAL THINKING AND *CHARACTERISTICS OF NEGRO EXPRESSION*

Primary critical thinking skill: EVALUATION
Secondary critical thinking skill: CREATIVE THINKING

The racial prejudices of 1930s America were many, and included a common presumption that African American art was unoriginal – merely poorly copying white culture.

African-American novelist, anthropologist and essayist Zora Neale Hurston crushingly evaluated such assumptions in her 1934 essay 'Characteristics of Negro Expression.' While Hurston's approach and premises seem in many ways dated to modern readers, the essay still shows an incisive mind carefully evaluating arguments and cutting them down to size. African-American art of the time did not – Hurston influentially argued – play by the same rules as white art, so it could not meaningfully be discussed by 'white' notions of aesthetic value.

Where white European tradition views art as something fixed, Hurston saw African-American art works as a distinctive form of mimicry, reshaping and altering the original object until it became something new and novel. In this way, she contended, African-American creative expression is a process that generates its own form of originality – turning borrowed material into something original and unique. By carefully evaluating the relevance of previous arguments, Hurston showed African American artistic expression in an entirely new light.

ABOUT THE AUTHOR OF THE ORIGINAL WORK

Novelist, essayist, and anthropologist **Zora Neale Hurston** was born in 1891 and raised in the all-black town of Eatonville, Florida. She won a scholarship to Barnard College in New York City, where she was the only black student, and researched African American folklore. Hurston also became part of the Harlem Renaissance, a flowering of African American arts and culture in the 1920s and 1930s. Her essay, 'Characteristics of Negro Expression,' was published in 1934, but Hurston's prominence waned during the 1940s, and when she died in 1960 she was buried in an unmarked grave. Interest in her work revived in the 1970s, however, and she is now considered one of America's greatest writers.

ABOUT THE AUTHORS OF THE ANALYSIS

Dr Mercedes Aguirre holds a PhD in American literature from University College, London. She is currently Curator of North American Published Collections at the British Library.

Dr Ben Lempert holds a PhD in rhetoric from the University of California at Berkeley for his research on form and voice in post-war American jazz and poetry. He has held a postdoctoral fellowship at Stanford and his research interests focus on the idea of "race" as it plays out in poetry, music, and fiction. Dr Lempert currently teaches college courses on literature, film, music, and writing.

ABOUT MACAT

GREAT WORKS FOR CRITICAL THINKING

Macat is focused on making the ideas of the world's great thinkers accessible and comprehensible to everybody, everywhere, in ways that promote the development of enhanced critical thinking skills.

It works with leading academics from the world's top universities to produce new analyses that focus on the ideas and the impact of the most influential works ever written across a wide variety of academic disciplines. Each of the works that sit at the heart of its growing library is an enduring example of great thinking. But by setting them in context – and looking at the influences that shaped their authors, as well as the responses they provoked – Macat encourages readers to look at these classics and game-changers with fresh eyes. Readers learn to think, engage and challenge their ideas, rather than simply accepting them.

'Macat offers an amazing first-of-its-kind tool for
interdisciplinary learning and research. Its focus on works
that transformed their disciplines and its rigorous approach,
drawing on the world's leading experts and educational institutions,
opens up a world-class education to anyone.'

Andreas Schleicher
Director for Education and Skills, Organisation for Economic
Co-operation and Development

'Macat is taking on some of the major challenges in university
education … They have drawn together a strong team of active
academics who are producing teaching materials that are
novel in the breadth of their approach.'

Prof Lord Broers,
former Vice-Chancellor of the University of Cambridge

'The Macat vision is exceptionally exciting. It focuses
upon new modes of learning which analyse and explain seminal texts
which have profoundly influenced world thinking and so social and
economic development. It promotes the kind of critical thinking
which is essential for any society and economy.
This is the learning of the future.'

Rt Hon Charles Clarke, former UK Secretary of State for Education

'The Macat analyses provide immediate access to the critical
conversation surrounding the books that have shaped their
respective discipline, which will make them an invaluable resource
to all of those, students and teachers, working in the field.'

Professor William Tronzo, University of California at San Diego

WAYS IN TO THE TEXT

KEY POINTS

- Zora Neale Hurston (1891–1960) was an African American author often associated with the Harlem Renaissance,* an artistic and social movement from the 1920s and 1930s, largely centered on the Harlem* neighborhood of New York City. Though most famous for her fiction, Hurston was also an accomplished folklorist* (a person who studies traditional local stories) and anthropologist* (a person who studies humankind).

- "Characteristics of Negro Expression" (1934) is an essay describing black expression as a powerful form of artistry that operates through creative mimicry*—that is, through the imitation of some aspect of art or language altered to create something new. It provides a framework for understanding how black culture works, and how African Americans interact with the world.

- While the essay functions as an anthropological record of black cultural expression, it also attempts to use the ways of expression it describes.

Who Was Zora Neale Hurston?

Zora Neale Hurston, the author of the essay "Characteristics of Negro Expression," was born in Notasulga, Alabama, in 1891, and her family moved to Eatonville,* Florida, while she was a toddler. Eatonville was one of the first US all-black incorporated* towns (a town with a state charter and elected officials). Hurston's father was a carpenter and Baptist* preacher (the Baptist Church is a Christian denomination that emphasizes the importance of the Christian sacrament of baptism); he later became Eatonville's mayor.

In 1918, Hurston began studying at Howard University in Washington, DC. There she became a member of the African American writer and educator Alain Locke's* literary club. In 1925 she won a scholarship to Barnard College in New York City, where she was the only black student; afterwards, she spent two years as a graduate student at Columbia University, also in New York. While she was there, Hurston began ethnographic* research (detailed study made "in the field") on African American folklore under the guidance of the famous anthropologist Franz Boas.* This research would later influence "Characteristics," published in 1934, and her book *Mules and Men*, published in 1935.

In the 1920s, Hurston became a fixture in the movement later known as the "Harlem Renaissance." She befriended many black luminaries, including the poet Langston Hughes* and the singer and actress Ethel Waters.* In 1937 she published what is now considered her fictional masterwork, *Their Eyes Were Watching God*. Hurston went on to write two more novels, an autobiography, and another work of non-fiction.

After her death in 1960 at the age of 69, Hurston's fame declined, and most of her texts fell out of print, but in the 1970s, interest in her work revived, due in part to the author Alice Walker* and her efforts to reclaim Hurston's memory and contribution. Today Hurston is widely considered one of the most important American authors of the twentieth century.

What Does "Characteristics of Negro Expression" Say?

In the essay, Hurston outlines the defining features of African American cultural expression. Black expression, she says, is more about *how* things are done than *what* is done. It is a process of imitation and reimagination. To Hurston, black culture "lives and moves in the midst of white civilization."[1] Yet it borrows and reworks the elements of white culture in a subtle and creative way.

"Characteristics" was published at a time when black artists and intellectuals, including the social theorist W. E. B. Du Bois* and Langston Hughes, were debating the role that art should play in the black community. Some people, like the publisher William Stanley Braithwaite,* thought black art should emphasize the viewpoint of the black middle class. "Characteristics," however, finds the essence of black artistry in the rural black cultures of the American South. As a trained anthropologist, Hurston based much of the essay on black folklore she collected through her ethnographic research in the South in 1927 and 1928. The essay includes analyses of language, dance, gesture, religion, storytelling, sexuality, and music. These examples aim to show how black people mimic art or language not out of a sense of inferiority but "for the love of it."[2] While this mimicry may seem garish or imitative to white observers, it reveals a way of interacting with the world—one in which "every hour of life"[3] provides opportunities for artistic expression.

The essay argues that black expression actively shapes American culture generally. For example, African American language pervades American speech. American music, she argues, is mostly black music. To Hurston, culture should be understood as a combination of influences. She calls this "the exchange and re-exchange of ideas between groups."[4]

Hurston describes black folklore as a living thing rather than a fixed set of stories. "It is still in the making,"[5] she argues. Given this, the essay not only collects black expression, but doubles as a *performance* of black expression, as Hurston adapts the scientific conventions of ethnographic research for her own creative and personal ends. "Characteristics" also recontextualizes the black cultural expressions

11

she collects, translating them for a new audience. Hurston presents the essay's information in a singular fashion, demonstrating the remaking of culture that she describes.

Why Does "Characteristics of Negro Expression" Matter?

"Characteristics" was one of the first essays to systematically study black cultural expression. It was also one of the first attempts to argue for the value of mimicry as an African American mode of expression. In so doing, the essay suggests that black expression is better understood as an ongoing expression of a particular artistic process. As such, Hurston's examples reveal an attitude towards the world rather than a set of fixed patterns.

Because of this dynamic, the essay remains an important theoretical document for understanding African American art forms of all kinds, including dance, literature, folklore, music, and religious expression. Though the essay was not widely read when it was first published, many scholars have since developed its ideas. In particular, "Characteristics" defended the artistic worth of black folklore and African American vernacular* culture (its informal spoken language or slang). It fixes the most important aspects of African American cultural identity in the rural South.

During the Harlem Renaissance of the 1920s and 1930s many black writers, including the novelist and essayist Richard Wright* and W. E. B. Du Bois, worried that vernacular art reinforced negative stereotypes. "Characteristics" brings Hurston's anthropological training into this heated debate, using many examples to show how the black vernacular in fact reveals a highly unique form of artistry. Today, scholars read the essay as a key thesis of the period, complementing the work of artists and theorists such as Langston Hughes, Alain Locke, and the politically conservative writer George Schuyler.*

The essay has both historical and theoretical importance. It clarifies the different critical trends of the Harlem Renaissance, while providing several lenses through which to view Hurston's own fiction. From a theoretical standpoint, "Characteristics" represents an important moment for understanding black aesthetic* theory (the attempt to determine what black art is, how it works, and what it means). It provides a crucial argument as to what an African American world view might be. In the years that have followed, many of the essay's themes have been applied to various other African American artistic endeavors. These run from the politically radical literature of the Black Arts Movement* in the late 1960s to discussions about hip-hop* music from the 1990s onwards.

Finally, we can also read the essay as a hybrid text that captures a tension between Hurston's dual roles as anthropologist and artist—and as a result creating imaginative art of its own.

NOTES

1   Zora Neale Hurston, "Characteristics of Negro Expression," in *Within the Circle: An Anthology of African American Literary Criticism From the Harlem Renaissance to the Present*, ed. Angelyn Mitchell (Durham, NC: Duke University Press, 1994), 86.

2   Hurston, "Characteristics of Negro Expression," 87.

3   Hurston, "Characteristics of Negro Expression," 79.

4   Hurston, "Characteristics of Negro Expression," 86.

5   Hurston, "Characteristics of Negro Expression," 84.

SECTION 1
INFLUENCES

MODULE 1
THE AUTHOR AND THE HISTORICAL CONTEXT

KEY POINTS

- Hurston's childhood in Eatonville,* Florida, gave her experiences with black cultural expression that she would turn to again and again in her work.

- "Characteristics of Negro Expression" tackles head-on many of the debates of the artistic and social movement known as the Harlem Renaissance,* especially those that concern representation and authenticity.

- Much of Hurston's work captures a tension she felt between being an anthropologist* and a black artist.

Why Read This Text?

"Characteristics of Negro Expression" is a seminal text of African American criticism in which Zora Neale Hurston, one of the most famous African American writers of the twentieth century, presents an aesthetic* theory of black cultural expression based on her anthropological fieldwork on black communities of the American South. The essay offers a powerful argument for the originality of black cultural expression and provides a new theoretical framework through which to understand African American art.

Most notably, the essay makes an extensive case for the role and value of mimicry* (the act of imitating some aspect of art or language and altering it to create something new), which Hurston cites as the key component of African American artistic expression. This claim has far-reaching implications, the most powerful being Hurston's definition of "originality" as "the modification of ideas."[1] By doing

> ❝ It was only when I was off in college, away from my native surroundings, that I could see myself like somebody else and stand off and look at my garment. Then I had to have the spy-glass of Anthropology to look through at that. ❞
>
> Zora Neale Hurston, *Mules and Men*

this, Hurston changes the standard of measurement used for evaluating black cultural expression. This not only vindicates the importance of black folklore language and music, but also shows how black artistry developed in the middle of white civilization.

Today the text is most valued for its contributions to literary and cultural studies, though it also makes important arguments concerning anthropology, linguistics (scientific inquiry into the nature of structures of language), folklore, and art. Often read as an important touchstone in the ongoing attempt to theorize black culture, the essay also provides insight into the debates of the Harlem Renaissance of the 1920s and 1930s, many of which hold relevance today.

Author's Life

Zora Neale Hurston was born in Alabama in 1891, but moved to Eatonville, Florida, while still a toddler. Eatonville was one of the first officially self-governed African American towns in the US. Growing up in a place governed entirely by black people clearly had a profound effect on Hurston, as she returned to Eatonville again and again in her fiction and anthropological work.

Her mother died when Hurston was 14 and she soon left home. After spending years wandering around, she eventually found herself in Baltimore where, at the age of 26, she lied about her age and finished high school. Soon after, she began attending Howard University and in 1924 had a short story accepted by *Opportunity*,* one of the important magazines of the movement now known as the Harlem Renaissance. This compelled her to move to New York in 1925, where she quickly became part of that movement. As one biographer, Valerie Boyd, notes, Hurston's personality often assisted her: "By all accounts … Hurston possessed a quality that enabled her to walk into a roomful of strangers and, a few minutes and a few stories later, leave them so completely charmed and so utterly impressed that they sometimes found themselves offering to help her in any way they could."[2]

While in New York, Hurston became interested in anthropology and soon won a scholarship to Barnard College, where she studied with the renowned anthropologist Franz Boas.* Under Boas's direction, Hurston returned to Eatonville in 1927 on a research trip to collect black folklore; in 1928 and 1929 she conducted similar ethnographic* research in Alabama, New Orleans, and the Bahamas. These studies formed the basis for both "Characteristics" and her book of folklore, *Mules and Men* (1935). Her ethnographic material would also find its way into her fiction, including the novels *Jonah's Gourd Vine* (1934) and *Their Eyes Were Watching God* (1937).

As she grew older, Hurston found it difficult to make a living. Her first biographer, Robert Hemenway, observes that "in 1950 she was discovered working as a maid on the same day one of her stories appeared in the *Saturday Evening Post*."[3] Hurston died in 1960 and was buried in an unmarked grave in Fort Pierce, Florida.

Author's Background

As a black woman from rural Eatonville, a trained anthropologist, a published novelist, and a Barnard-educated academic, Hurston often felt caught between identities. Much of her work captures this tension. While other black intellectuals in her New York circle asserted that black culture was best embodied in the practices of its rural folk, few had actual experience with this culture. Hurston, in contrast, had come from a poor background in the South. On the one hand, this gave her an advantage in that her accounts of black vernacular* expression were culled from her life experiences. On the other hand, her academic background often distanced her from that culture, forcing her to objectify it. In her first ethnographic trip to Eatonville, she explains by way of example, "I knew where the material was … but, I went about asking, in carefully accented Barnardese, 'Pardon me, but do you know any folk tales or folk songs?'"[4]

She also worried about writing down the stories of a folk culture whose essence was improvisational rather than fixed. As a result, Hurston's work often mixed her academic and her artistic practices: she created novels based on folklore, academic studies that incorporated material from her stories, and an autobiography generally considered more fictional than true.

NOTES

1   Zora Neale Hurston, "Characteristics of Negro Expression," in *Within the Circle: An Anthology of African American Literary Criticism From the Harlem Renaissance to the Present*, ed. Angelyn Mitchell (Durham, NC: Duke University Press, 1994), 86.

2   Valerie Boyd, *Wrapped in Rainbows: The Life of Zora Neale Hurston* (New York: Scribner, 2003), 99.

3   Robert E. Hemenway, *Zora Neale Hurston: A Literary Biography* (Urbana: University of Illinois Press, 1977), 4.

4   Zora Neale Hurston, *Dust Tracks on a Road* (New York: HarperPerennial, 1996), 144.

MODULE 2
ACADEMIC CONTEXT

KEY POINTS

- Black aesthetic* theory attempts to explain how specific artworks or styles of art-making articulate something important about African American experience.

- The writer and political activist Frederick Douglass* and the social theorist W. E. B. Du Bois,* writing in the late nineteenth and early twentieth century, developed early versions of African American aesthetic theory, though debates on black art would continue through the artistic and social movement known as the Harlem Renaissance* to the present day.

- Hurston's essay implements many ideas developed by her teacher, the pioneering anthropologist* Franz Boas*— albeit with a personal spin.

The Work in its Context

"Characteristics of Negro Expression" was one of six essays Zora Neale Hurston contributed to the British writer and activist Nancy Cunard's* *Negro: An Anthology* (1934), a collection of criticism, literature, and art by and about African Americans. Unfortunately, *Negro*'s size—more than 800 pages—made it expensive to produce and only 1,000 copies were printed. As a result, "Characteristics" was not discussed in depth until Cunard's anthology was reprinted in 1970.

Scholars today consider "Characteristics" a critical document in the tradition of black aesthetic theory, though it was barely read on first publication. Black aesthetic theory attempts to describe the unique characteristics of African American art. It began in the mid-

> ❝ Still, the chief part of the negro music is *civilized* in
> its character—partly composed under the influence
> of association with the whites, partly actually imitated
> from their music. In the main it appears to be original
> in the best sense of the word, and the more we examine
> the subject, the more genuine it appears to us to be. ❞
>
> William Francis Allen, Charles Pickard Ware, and Lucy McKim Garrison,
> *Slave Songs of the United States*

nineteenth century, and often responded to black stereotypes that
pervaded American culture at that time. In the minstrel show,* a
popular form of entertainment, white performers painted their faces
black and lampooned blacks as "slow-talking, slow-walking, self-
demeaning [nitwits]."[1] Similarly, literature with black characters often
depicted black dialect* as impossibly difficult to understand. In the
scientific world, phrenology* (the now-discredited study of the size
and shape of the head, then considered a legitimate mode of inquiry)
asserted the natural inferiority of "the Negro."

In the face of these stereotypes and false assumptions, African
American and white writers began to defend the uniqueness and
power of black artistry. Frederick Douglass, an ex-slave who became
one of the most famous Americans of the nineteenth century, was an
early and powerful voice in this movement. W. E. B. Du Bois carried
these ideas forward in his work *The Souls of Black Folk* (1903). But the
greatest flowering of the idea that black art possessed value came with
the Harlem Renaissance,* a period when black creativity gained
national and worldwide recognition.

Overview of the Field

"Characteristics" builds on the work of numerous predecessors, most
prominently Douglass and Du Bois. Importantly, both men argued

that two features best characterized African American art: *improvisation*—unscripted work created in the moment—and *mimesis*—creatively imitated material taken from the outside world.

In his *Narrative* (1845), for example, Douglass describes slaves singing, characterizing their actions as more about *process* than *product*:"they would compose and sing as they went along, consulting neither time nor tune."[2] Douglass also emphasizes their improvisatory character: "the thought that came up, came out—if not in the word, in the sound,"[3] he notes. He further describes how music that sounded primitive in fact carried a deeper truth: "they would sing words which to many would seem unmeaning jargon, but which, nevertheless were full of meaning to themselves."[4]

Du Bois—sociologist, philosopher, historian, fiction writer, activist, and editor—built on Douglass's account in his landmark book *The Souls of Black Folk*. Du Bois developed a theory of black psychology in his idea of "double consciousness,*"[5] a theory that describes African American identity as an inner conflict between two identities: "American" and "Negro."[6] Though borne simultaneously, the two are at odds with each other, given that the former views the latter with contempt. Importantly, Du Bois also describes mimicry as a defining characteristic of "Negro" expression. In describing Negro spirituals* (Christian hymns of the African American tradition) he argues that "things evidently borrowed from the surrounding world undergo characteristic change when they enter the mouth of the slave."[7]

Du Bois also introduces the idea—later echoed by Hurston—that African American culture, as the only culture born and raised on American soil, should be seen as emblematic of America as a whole. White culture, by contrast, represented an extension of Europe, while Native American culture had been wiped out by conquest. "There is," he wrote, "no true American music but the wild sweet melodies of the Negro slave."[8]

Academic Influences

Hurston's major academic influence was her anthropologist mentor Franz Boas, a scholar often called the "Father of American Anthropology. " Years before Hurston became his student, Boas worked to rid the field of "scientific racism."* He argued against the prominent anthropological view, held by the British scientist and philosopher Herbert Spencer and others, that biological features such as head size could account for variances in intelligence, contending instead that racial difference was a *social* not a biological phenomenon. In countering cultural anthropologists—those engaged in the study of human societies—who ranked cultures on a scale of "civilization," Boas asserted that cultures could only be understood on their own terms. He thought, like George Hutchinson,* a prominent scholar of the Harlem Renaissance, that "all cultures are, in the final analysis, mixed."[9]

Boas also proved influential in the study of folklore, believing that it best uncovered the values held by different cultures. As his student, Hurston (who called him "Papa Boas") remained committed to these views, and many traces of them can be seen in "Characteristics"—including her insistence that black expression be evaluated according to its own aims, and her belief in the living power of folklore. She filters Boas's ideas, however, through her personal stories and point of view. These turn "Characteristics" into a document that not only describes folk culture, but also *becomes* a vital expression of that culture.

NOTES

1   David Pilgrim, "The Coon Caricature," *Jim Crow Museum of Racist Memorabilia* (2012), accessed November 25, 2015, http://www.ferris.edu/news/jimcrow/coon/.

2   Frederick Douglass, *Narrative of the Life of Frederick Douglass, an American Slave,* ed. John W. Blassingame, John R. McKivigan, and Peter P. Hinks (New Haven, CT: Yale University Press, 2001), 20.

3   Douglass, *Narrative of the Life of Frederick Douglass*, 20.

4   Douglass, *Narrative of the Life of Frederick Douglass*, 20.

5   W. E. B. Du Bois, *The Souls of Black Folk* (New York: Penguin Books, 1996), 5.

6   Du Bois, *The Souls of Black Folk*, 5.

7   Du Bois, *The Souls of Black Folk*, 212.

8   Du Bois, *The Souls of Black Folk*, 12.

9   George Hutchinson, *The Harlem Renaissance in Black and White*
     (Cambridge, MA: Harvard University Press, 1995), 67.

MODULE 3
THE PROBLEM

KEY POINTS

- "Characteristics" asks whether a recognizable mode of African American art exists—but in so doing, answers a number of much larger questions.

- Hurston agreed in part with many other intellectuals of her time, including the poet Langston Hughes,* the social theorist W. E. B. Du Bois,* and the critic Alain Locke,* but stakes her own ground in these debates.

- While Hurston was active in the artistic movement known as the Harlem Renaissance,* her work was less influential at the time than it would be in later years.

Core Question

The principal question taken up in Zora Neale Hurston's 1934 essay "Characteristics of Negro Expression" revolved around whether there existed an original black art that did not merely copy or react to white American culture. Hurston wrote the essay at the tail end of a period known as "the Harlem Renaissance," a movement that arguably represented the most concentrated period of African American artistic output in US history. Yet as much as the Harlem Renaissance represented a sustained and focused artistic effort, it also sparked heated (if productive) intellectual dispute about how African American art should look, whom it should serve, and what its relationship to politics should be. As the Harlem Renaissance scholar George Hutchinson* writes in his study of the period, "Never before had there been such variety or productivity, or so much critical dissensus."[1]

> **❝** Therefore, the Negro today wishes to be known for what he is, even in his faults and shortcomings, and scorns a craven and precarious survival at the price of seeming to be what he is not. **❞**
>
> Alain Locke, "Enter the New Negro"

In arguing for the importance of Negro folklore, Hurston engaged a much larger set of questions. The most prominent were perhaps:

- Which criteria will best help readers—both black and white— understand the unique African American experience?
- Which aspects of African American expressive culture can be seen as truly authentic?

The Participants

Today we celebrate the Harlem Renaissance for its lasting art forms, notably jazz music and the poetry of Langston Hughes—but often overlook how divisive these artworks were, and how they catalyzed impassioned debates. As Hutchinson describes: "African American intellectuals took a number of strong positions on intellectual standards; but they did not agree on what those standards should be."[2] Most believed that, as Alain Locke put it, "for generations … the Negro has been more of a formula than a human being."[3] Yet there was little concordance about how to remedy this situation.

Hughes, for example, took a position similar to Hurston's, arguing that African American artists had too long aspired to be seen as "proper" by white society. As a result, black artists had avoided the "wealth of colorful, distinctive material" that comes from "the low-down folks, the so-called common element." Therefore, his call to utilize this "great field of unused material"[4] argued that there is artistic *content* that is authentically black. Alain Locke, in contrast, called for more individualistic expression. "Art in the best sense is rooted in self-expression and whether naive or sophisticated is self-contained,"[5] he wrote, arguing that this, rather than prescribed content, helped art reach a wider audience.

W. E. B. Du Bois agreed that African American artists were expected to conform to negative stereotypes: "Uncle Toms,* Topsies, good 'darkies' and clowns."[6] Yet he concluded that "all art is propaganda"[7] and that "the art of black folk" should work to "[compel] recognition"[8] from wider society. More conservative claims came from the author George Schuyler,* who argued that "it is sheer nonsense to talk about 'racial differences' as between the American black man and the American white man."[9]

"Characteristics" stakes out its own ground. Hurston follows Hughes in emphasizing vernacular expression, but distances herself from Hughes's use of "they"—which implied a separation between him and the common people. Hurston's background makes this alleged divide irrelevant. While she supports Locke by arguing that all vernacular expression is personal, she also holds that African American expression possesses inherent characteristics distinct from those of white artistry. In opposition to Du Bois and Schuyler, Hurston argues that black artists should use recognizable vernacular content.

The Contemporary Debate

When "Characteristics" was published in 1934, Hurston was unknown outside of her circle of Harlem* acquaintances and yet to publish the fiction that would make her famous. She was still assembling *Mules and Men* (1935), her major book of folklore that the folklorist and music collector Alan Lomax* would later call "the most engaging, genuine, and skillfully written book in the field of folklore."[10] She was, however, an active member of Harlem's intellectual scene, had won many literary awards alongside Hughes and the poet Countee Cullen,* and was friends with Du Bois and Locke. Yet despite her active engagement with the movement, she would also come to know her share of disillusionment. By the end of the 1920s, she had become great friends with Langston Hughes, and in 1930 they began collaborating on a humorous play entitled *Mule Bone*. However, for reasons still unknown, though scholars believe involved either literary patronage or romantic jealousy, the two broke off their friendship and would never speak again. *Mule Bone* was finally performed on Broadway in 1991.

In fact, Hurston would not enjoy widespread acclaim or influence in her lifetime. She died in 1960, but it would not be until the 1970s that her work would begin to be read as offering a major contribution to African American thought and art.

NOTES

1   George Hutchinson, *The Harlem Renaissance in Black and White* (Cambridge, MA: Harvard University Press, 1995), 17.

2   Hutchinson, *The Harlem Renaissance in Black and White*, 17.

3   Alain Locke, "The New Negro," in *The Portable Harlem Renaissance Reader*, ed. David Levering Lewis (New York: Viking Penguin, 1994), 47.

4   Langston Hughes, "The Negro Artist and the Racial Mountain," in *The Portable Harlem Renaissance Reader*, ed. David Levering Lewis (New York: Viking Penguin, 1994), 92.

5   Alain Locke, "Art Or Propaganda?" in *Voices of the Harlem Renaissance*, ed. Nathan Irvin Huggins (New York: Oxford University Press, 1976), 312.

6   W. E. B. Du Bois, "Criteria of Negro Art," in *The Portable Harlem Renaissance Reader*, ed. David Levering Lewis (New York: Viking Penguin, 1994), 102.

7   Du Bois, "Criteria of Negro Art," 103.

8   Du Bois, "Criteria of Negro Art," 104.

9   George Schuyler, "The Negro-Art Hokum," in *The Portable Harlem Renaissance Reader*, ed. David Levering Lewis (New York: Viking Penguin, 1994), 98.

10 Robert E. Hemenway, *Zora Neale Hurston: A Literary Biography* (Urbana: University of Illinois Press, 1977), 6.

MODULE 4
THE AUTHOR'S CONTRIBUTION

KEY POINTS

- In "Characteristics" Zora Neale Hurston aimed to provide a framework for understanding African American culture, and in turn to vindicate its originality.

- Hurston turned the essay itself into a work of black cultural expression, making it an extension of the folkloric style she describes.

- "Characteristics" builds most directly on the author and social theorist W. E. B. Du Bois's* *The Souls of Black Folk*, but its anthropological* framework is also directed at Hurston's interlocutors and fellow artists in the Harlem Renaissance.*

Author's Aims

Zora Neale Hurston begins "Characteristics of Negro Expression" by arguing that mimicry,* a "universal" feature of African American culture, is not a "thing in itself" but "evidence of something that pervades [the] entire self."[1] Mimicry is not, she notes, a behavior a "Negro" can take on and off like a piece of clothing. Instead, it signals a deeper world view that sees all elements of the world as potential material for creative imitation.

Hurston's first aim in the essay is to explain this world view and use it to properly contextualize black cultural expression. She contends that, in order to understand what makes such expression beneficial, one must view it through the values of the African American community itself. This helps explain her choice of examples, many taken from arenas not always considered worthy of artistic evaluation: slang, home decorating, religion, street-corner drama, and folklore.

66 She entered unto the homely life of the southern
Negro as one of them and was fully accepted as such by
the companions of her childhood. Thus she has been able
to penetrate through that affected demeanor by which
the Negro excludes the white observer effectively from
participating in his true inner life. 99

Franz Boas,* Preface to *Mules and Men*

For Hurston, the fact that African Americans view all these contexts as
opportunities for creativity shows how the desire to create pervades
the whole of black life, rather than just a few select areas.

Her second aim is to properly transcribe African American speech.
Before 1930, the major written record of ostensibly black language
existed in the dialect* fiction of white writers such as Octavus Roy
Cohen* and Roark Bradford,* who depicted the dialect as defective
rather than creative. "Characteristics" intended, as the English professor
and literary critic Michael North* puts it, "to take back a language
obscured by travesty and stereotype, so negatively charged that
educated blacks were afraid to use it"[2]—and in turn donate this
language to her literary peers for artistic uses.

Approach
"Characteristics" stands out for mixing personal, literary, and academic
components in a strategy that allows the essay itself to enact the form
of creative imitation it describes. It lists facets of African American
cultural expression in mini-sections that often shift in focus. Yet this
structure conforms to the essay's descriptions of what characterizes
African American art: "abrupt and unexpected changes,"[3] "rhythm of
segments,"[4] and "dynamic suggestion."[5]

At the heart of this approach lies the black folklore Hurston
collected on her ethnographic* trips to the American South in the

late 1920s. Hurston, however, acted as more than an anthropologist;* she also participated in the folk culture she recorded. Rather than offering objective, distanced reporting, Hurston inserts herself into the narrative, recounting black folklore from her personal perspective. Conceptually, this strategy transforms her from an objective chronicler into a cultural intermediary—one who keeps folklore and stories alive by showing rather than telling.

This squares with Hurston's assertion that "Negro folklore is not a thing of the past. It is still in the making."[6] In using her descriptions of black cultural expression to make a new point about them, Hurston employs creative mimicry to revise American cultural narratives. This mimicry is structural and conceptual—it rewrites how anthropology presented and accepted notions of black inferiority.

Contribution in Context

Structurally, Hurston's essay owes much to W. E. B. Du Bois's *The Souls of Black Folk* (1903). Like Hurston's essay, Du Bois's book is both a collection of smaller portraits and an anthology of black cultural productions. Each chapter of *Souls* opens with a piece of sheet music from a Negro spiritual,* presented without words, that creates a kind of "dynamic suggestion" about black art, to borrow Hurston's words. Du Bois also blends the personal, scientific, and fictional in his book, generating, as Michael North writes, "a collection of miscellaneous pieces that aspires to be a collective portrait of a people."[7]

Like Du Bois, Hurston blends all of these approaches as a means to establish her authority as an accredited translator of black folkloric material. Raised as middle class in the northern United States, Du Bois gained this authority by traveling to the South. Yet Hurston was able to claim it from birth: she grew up listening to folklore being created on the porches of Eatonville.* As a result, both the structure and method of Hurston's essay allow her to employ and even perform this authority for multiple audiences: white academics, black northern intellectuals, *and* southern rural folk. Indeed, when Hurston says "we may go to the Negro and let him speak for himself,"[8] the "Negro" in this phrase not only refers to those whose speech Hurston has transcribed, it refers to Hurston herself.

NOTES

1   Zora Neale Hurston, "Characteristics of Negro Expression," in *Within the Circle: An Anthology of African American Literary Criticism From the Harlem Renaissance to the Present*, ed. Angelyn Mitchell (Durham, NC: Duke University Press, 1994), 79.

2   Michael North, *The Dialect of Modernism: Race, Language, and Twentieth-Century Literature* (New York: Oxford University Press, 1998), 176.

3   Hurston, "Characteristics of Negro Expression," 83.

4   Hurston, "Characteristics of Negro Expression," 84.

5   Hurston, "Characteristics of Negro Expression," 84.

6   Hurston, "Characteristics of Negro Expression," 84.

7   North, *The Dialect of Modernism*, 185.

8   Hurston, "Characteristics of Negro Expression," 92.

SECTION 2
IDEAS

MODULE 5
MAIN IDEAS

KEY POINTS

- "Characteristics" focuses on the idea of mimicry,* which Hurston sees as the critical mode of African American cultural expression, and a process of art-making rather than a specific set of artworks.

- In making this point, Hurston offers a larger argument that puts mimicry at the center of art in general.

- Hurston's analysis of African American language both names and performs the process of creative mimicry.

Key Themes

In "Characteristics of Negro Expression," Zora Neale Hurston argues that African American expression is highly original and creative. This expression is fundamentally rooted in what she calls "mimicry." For Hurston, "mimicry" does not indicate the simple copying of actions taken from non–African American cultures; rather, it indicates the "treatment of borrowed material,"[1] that is, the transformation of outside material into something unique.

This process of mimicry, she points out, can take any number of forms. The essay provides examples from many different areas of life—language, decoration, music, religion, poetry, folklore, dance, and sexuality. Yet Hurston divides the essay into sections that describe processes rather than genres of art. Her first section, for example, is entitled "Drama"—but "drama" turns out to mean "adorned," or exaggerated in a creative way. In addition to the theatrical connotation, "drama" encompasses language, metaphor, and simile; even "theater" here has an expanded definition, referring to all interpersonal interactions.

❝ If we look at it squarely, the Negro is a very original being. While he lives and moves in the midst of a white civilization, everything he touches is re-interpreted for his own use. ❞

Zora Neale Hurston, "Characteristics of Negro Expression"

The second section, "Will to Adorn," likewise incorporates black slang, home decorating, and sermons. Other descriptive sections include "Angularity" (the avoidance of "the simple straight line"[2]), "Asymmetry" (examples of which are poetry and dance), "Originality," and "Imitation."

These all point to the fact that Hurston sees African American creative expression as based on *process* rather than *product*. It does not necessarily matter to the African American community *what* is imitated—indeed, there is no aspect of life that is not ripe for imitation—but *how* that thing is imitated: whether the imitation produces a meaning that did not exist before.

Exploring the Ideas

Hurston's description of African American imitation involves a number of consequences. These begin with her radical redefinition of what counts as "originality." While the European art tradition, in biographer Robert Hemenway's words, "conceives of art as something fixed,"[3] to Hurston this understanding is flawed. Indeed, Hurston points out that the first examples of human expression are untraceable. As a result, *all* art necessarily works through creative imitation. Originality should therefore be seen as "the modification of ideas,"[4] with the most original artist, in the words of the English professor Michael North, being "the one who most thoroughly modifies."[5] In this account, art is not a fixed thing but an ongoing process, "still in the making."[6]

What's more, Hurston finds the widespread "contention that the Negro imitates from a feeling of inferiority"[7] completely wrong. African Americans engage in imitation not because they want to belong to the culture they imitate; "the Negro" imitates because mimicry "permeates his entire self."[8] To Hurston, mimicry is fundamental to the cultural outlook that defines what it is to be "Negro."

While black culture "lives and moves in the middle of white civilization,"[9] the most impressive part of this culture is how it has carved out a space for itself within that civilization. In discussing folklore, for example, Hurston introduces Jack, a protagonist famous for outsmarting even God and the Devil. In Hurston's account, Jack is "the greatest cultural hero of the South,"[10] because he allegorizes African American culture as a whole, relying on his adaptability to survive amidst an antagonistic culture.

Language and Expression

"Characteristics" is a hybrid text that offers anthropological* and theoretical arguments, but often employs a first-person narrative that ties these academic analyses to Hurston's history as a fiction writer who grew up in the South. This emerges clearest in the essay's description of African American language. Hurston explains that the Negro "thinks in hieroglyphics"—words that invoke action instead of detached ideas. Yet the language that results enables a great many opportunities for creative expression. As an example, she lists "Negro" metaphors and similes, such as "regular as pig-tracks," or the use of "syndicating" as a synonym for "gossiping."[11] There are "Double Descriptives," which include phrases such as "chop-axe" and "low-down."[12] And there are also "Verbal Nouns," or verbs turned into nouns in expressions such as "she won't take a listen."[13]

That Hurston coins the categories "Double Descriptive" and "Verbal Nouns," however, subtly shows her modifying the language of linguistics in a way that mirrors how African American language modifies conventional English. Furthermore, the fact that metaphor and simile are defining attributes of black language suggests that Hurston's fiction itself grows from her childhood exposure to the town of Eatonville's* vernacular* culture—a rural, yet highly expressive language she mastered long before setting foot in a big-city college.

NOTES

1   Zora Neale Hurston, "Characteristics of Negro Expression," in *Within the Circle: An Anthology of African American Literary Criticism From the Harlem Renaissance to the Present*, ed. Angelyn Mitchell (Durham, NC: Duke University Press, 1994), 86.

2   Hurston, "Characteristics of Negro Expression," 83.

3   Robert E. Hemenway, *Zora Neale Hurston: A Literary Biography* (Urbana: University of Illinois Press, 1977),80–1.

4   Hurston, "Characteristics of Negro Expression," 86.

5   Michael North, *The Dialect of Modernism: Race, Language, and Twentieth-Century Literature* (New York: Oxford University Press, 1998), 182.

6   Hurston, "Characteristics of Negro Expression," 84.

7   Hurston, "Characteristics of Negro Expression," 87.

8   Hurston, "Characteristics of Negro Expression," 79.

9   Hurston, "Characteristics of Negro Expression," 87.

10 Hurston, "Characteristics of Negro Expression," 85.

11 Hurston, "Characteristics of Negro Expression," 81.

12 Hurston, "Characteristics of Negro Expression," 81.

13 Hurston, "Characteristics of Negro Expression," 82.

MODULE 6
SECONDARY IDEAS

KEY POINTS

- The two most important secondary ideas in "Characteristics" are that African American spirituals* have never been authentically performed for white audiences, and that white artists have failed to imitate "Negro" art correctly.

- Though these arguments are related, both imply the existence of broad misunderstanding of the true nature of African American art.

- Scholars now see Hurston's essay as potentially articulating what is now called an "essentialist*" notion of African American identity.

Other Ideas

One key secondary idea Zora Neale Hurston proposes in "Characteristics of Negro Expression" is that no authentic version of a Negro spiritual has ever been performed for a white audience. While Hurston expounds on this idea in her essay "Spirituals and Neo-Spirituals" (1934)—also published in Nancy Cunard's *Negro: An Anthology*—the fundamental thrust is that spirituals, like all African American art, are not fixed entities meant to be sung the same way every time. Instead, they represent a set of loose forms meant to enable an "expression of feelings" rather than "sound effects."[1] This claim stems from her larger argument that black art is a present, living process—not "a thing of the past" (even the very recent past), but "still in the making."[2]

A related idea is Hurston's argument that white performers have been so far unable to properly imitate African American art. In the 1920s, such attempts were legion: white musicians like Paul

> 66 In spite of the goings up and down on the earth, from the original Fisk Jubilee Singers to the present, there has been no genuine presentation of Negro songs to white audiences. 99
>
> Zora Neale Hurston, "Characteristics of Negro Expression"

Whiteman* were famous for playing jazz; popular black dances including the Charleston swept the country; and Al Jolson,* a white singer of African American songs who often performed in blackface* (in which white actors would wear black make-up and perform caricatured representations of black people), was one of the country's most popular entertainers. To Hurston, these performers failed to convey the most crucial element of "Negro" art.

Exploring the Ideas

Hurston's claim that spirituals had never been authentically performed for a white audience caused controversy. By the 1920s, black singing groups, including the Fisk Jubilee Singers* and Tuskegee Choir,* had toured the world for years, singing spirituals to wide acclaim, and generally to the pride of the African American community. But Hurston insists that these groups, by cleaning up arrangements and giving them regular harmonies, "spread a misconception of Negro spirituals."[3] Rather than being "final things,"[4] endlessly repeatable, real spirituals are defined by their endless mutability (changeableness): the fact that they are *not* meant to "remain long in their original form."[5] As a result, the only place to hear "the songs as the Negro song-makers sing them"[6] is in the "unfashionable Negro church."[7]

This idea helps us understand Hurston's critique of white artists who "seem to think that the Negro is easily imitated."[8] Hurston names many such artists: singer Mae West,* composer George Gershwin,* dancer Ann Pennington,* and the "white damsels who try to sing the blues."[9] Hurston describes their failures in terms of their performances, saying that their imitations are "distorted by the accent falling on the wrong element."[10] But her deeper implication is that these performers fall short because they, too, treat African American art as a set of fixed songs and movements, rather than an essentially *improvised* response to the world around it. Hurston implies that these artists miss the participatory aspect of African American art, whose proper context is the church, the street, or the porch—places where the point is conversation and interaction, rather than rigid performance.

Overlooked

Hurston's essay itself was almost entirely overlooked at the time of its publication. Although published in 1934, it took until the 1970s for it to gain a significant readership. In a deeper sense, it took until recent years for readers to acknowledge a key conceptual tension, foregrounded by her arguments about Negro spirituals, that animates Hurston's essay: If the essence of Negro art is impossible to capture in fixed form, then what are we to make of Hurston's transcriptions of Negro language and folklore? Do they also drain African American art of its essence? How can Hurston claim to represent and capture something untranslatable?

While the implications of Hurston's broader argument are now considered critical, these questions were not considered important or useful until "authenticity"* became an important concept in the 1980s. Today, however, scholars have used this element of Hurston's essay to launch their own theories about authenticity and African American identity. Some, such as Cheryl Wall, have offered answers by showing how Hurston's text creatively transforms Negro art into writing, and showcases the possibilities of this art for further transformation, rather than asserting that its examples are final and comprehensive.[11]

Others characterize Hurston's argument as offering an essentialist* notion of identity (the idea that certain forms of identity are entirely decided by essential properties such as race). The British cultural critic Paul Gilroy,* for example, cites it as an example of Hurston's desire to prescribe what counts as "authentically black,"[12] and the US critic Hazel Carby,* a scholar of African American literature and gender, similarly notes how "Hurston was concerned to establish authenticity in the representation of popular forms of folk culture."[13] That these readings emerged in the 1980s and 1990s suggests that it was only when scholars began to develop these concepts that they could be found at work in, if not animating, Hurston's essay.

NOTES

1 Zora Neale Hurston, "Spirituals and Neo-Spirituals," in *Negro: An Anthology*, ed. Nancy Cunard (New York: Continuum, 1996), 224.

2 Zora Neale Hurston, "Characteristics of Negro Expression," in *Within the Circle: An Anthology of African American Literary Criticism From the Harlem Renaissance to the Present*, ed. Angelyn Mitchell (Durham, NC: Duke University Press, 1994), 84.

3 Hurston, "Characteristics of Negro Expression," 93.

4 Hurston, "Spirituals and Neo-Spirituals," 224.

5 Hurston, "Spirituals and Neo-Spirituals," 223.

6 Hurston, "Characteristics of Negro Expression," 93.

7 Hurston, "Characteristics of Negro Expression," 93.

8 Hurston, "Characteristics of Negro Expression," 92.

9 Hurston, "Characteristics of Negro Expression," 92.

10 Hurston, "Characteristics of Negro Expression," 92.

11 Cheryl A. Wall, "Zora Neale Hurston's Essays: On Art and Such," *S&F Online* 3, no. 2 (2005), accessed November 25, 2015, http://sfonline.barnard.edu/hurston/wall_01.htm.

12 Paul Gilroy, *The Black Atlantic: Modernity and Double-Consciousness* (Cambridge, MA: Harvard University Press, 1993), 92.

13 Hazel V. Carby, "The Politics of Fiction, Anthropology, and the Folk: Zora Neale Hurston," in *New Essays on Their Eyes Were Watching God*, ed. Michael Awkward (Cambridge: Cambridge University Press, 1991), 75.

MODULE 7
ACHIEVEMENT

KEY POINTS

- "Characteristics" succeeds in conveying the meaning and importance of mimicry* for black expression. This success can be measured by how the essay leads us to understand American culture in a new way, as the exchange of ideas.

- While the essay was not well read at the time of its publication, Hurston successfully incorporated many of the ideas in "Characteristics" in her fiction, particularly her novel *Their Eyes Were Watching God* (1937).

- Two potential limitations of the essay include its endorsement of ideas of the "primitive," and the risk of "essentialism"* in her argument about Negro spirituals.*

Assessing the Argument

In the opening lines of "Characteristics of Negro Expression," Zora Neale Hurston reveals her primary purpose: to explore the implications of mimicry as the key element of African American expression. At the same time, the essay aims to document instances of black vernacular* expression in a way that does justice to their actual manifestations. It then aims to use these pieces of documentation to convey the world view Hurston believes is most authentically "Negro."

By most measures, the essay succeeds in the first of these intentions and Hurston's analysis of mimicry spells out several important implications. Most notably, it offers a new reading not only of African American culture but also of the United States more generally. By documenting instances of African American culture, Hurston shows how black culture has indelibly shaped the nation as a whole. She draws examples of this phenomenon from language and music.

> **❝** The most important African American literary modernists were those who were *both* more prone to interracial intimacy (despite its frequent cost) and most secure in their convictions about the cultural wealth of black America. **❞**
>
> George Hutchinson, *The Harlem Renaissance in Black and White*

Linguistically, for example, "no one listening to a Southern white man talk could deny"[1] the influence of black language on white speech. Music provides an even more compelling example. When the white jazz musician Paul Whiteman* performs, Hurston notes, he is "giving an imitation of a Negro orchestra making use of white-invented musical instruments in a Negro way."[2] If the chain of influence in this description seems confusing, that is exactly Hurston's point: *no* culture is pure. Civilization itself, Hurston argues, is "the exchange and re-exchange of ideas between groups,"[3] with America as the prime example.

Achievement in Context

"Characteristics" received little attention on first publication and was out of print until 1970. By then, cultural contexts had changed and the essay was seen as a historical document—more useful for understanding the artistic and social movement known as the Harlem Renaissance* and the lineage of black aesthetic theory* than for contributing to a contemporary debate.

However, the success of the ideas in "Characteristics" can be gauged, given that many play out in Hurston's fiction, particularly her most famous novel, *Their Eyes Were Watching God*, which devotes extensive space to depicting the creation of black vernacular expression. Capturing Hurston's idea that African American identity lies in its "universal mimicry,"[4] the book's narrative voice moves between conventional English and dialect.* In addition, key moments of personal growth for the book's main character, Janie, occur when she learns to participate in acts of linguistic creation that bind the black community in which she lives. The book now ranks as one of the most important American novels of the twentieth century, and has spawned many theories of African American expressive identity. This suggests that the ideas discussed in "Characteristics" proved influential—even if the essay itself did not become quite as influential until later.

Limitations

One major conceptual limitation in the essay concerns Hurston's intermittent characterization of black culture as "primitive."[5] At the time many accounts of "Negro" inferiority—particularly the so-called "scientific" investigations into head size and other physical features—asserted that the inferiority of African American people stemmed from African civilizations being more primitive than their European counterparts. Hurston's essay distinguishes between inferiority and primitivism. She clearly aims to refute the alleged inferiority of the Negro, but makes it less clear whether she also wants to reject the idea that the Negro is more primitive. Hurston could, in fact, be arguing that the Negro *is* primitive, and that being primitive is what enables his creativity. As one scholar puts it, what remains unclear is whether "Hurston is arguing that Negro people and Negro arts really *are* primitive but nonetheless powerful and compelling, or that beneath the face of the so-called primitive"[6] lies a more developed mode of artistic accomplishment.

How one approaches this question changes the political implications of the essay. The first answer forms an argument for *keeping* African Americans primitive, so as to protect their artistry from contamination. But the second implies that reading Negro artistic expressions as "primitive" simply reflects a superficial application of a modern mode of expression.

A related limitation emerges in Hurston's discussion of Negro spirituals,* which Hurston argues have never been performed authentically for a white audience. Indeed, one implication of this claim is that the purity of the spirituals—and by extension black culture as a whole—rests on the ongoing *isolation* of the African American community. This implies that even though American culture is built on the "exchange ... of ideas between groups,"[7] the essence of African American culture does not translate into different modes of performance. The political stakes of this argument are significant. If this idea of purity is taken seriously, one conclusion is that the health of African American culture requires an ongoing segregation of black and white cultures.

A powerful question arises about "Characteristics," which engages in its own translation of black culture into a more academic format. Does Hurston's translation *itself* also impinge on African American purity? The essay never answers this question, paving the way for a wide-ranging debate about its ultimate meaning.

NOTES

1   Zora Neale Hurston, "Characteristics of Negro Expression," in *Within the Circle: An Anthology of African American Literary Criticism From the Harlem Renaissance to the Present*, ed. Angelyn Mitchell (Durham, NC: Duke University Press, 1994), 80.

2   Hurston, "Characteristics of Negro Expression," 86.

3   Hurston, "Characteristics of Negro Expression," 86.

4   Hurston, "Characteristics of Negro Expression," 79.

5   Hurston, "Characteristics of Negro Expression," 79.

6   Karen Jacobs, *The Eye's Mind: Literary Modernism and Visual Culture* (Ithaca, NY: Cornell University Press, 2001), 123.

7   Hurston, "Characteristics of Negro Expression," 86.

MODULE 8
PLACE IN THE AUTHOR'S WORK

KEY POINTS

- "Characteristics" offers an intellectual bridge that links debates of the Harlem Renaissance* with the focus on black vernacular* expression that Zora Neale Hurston implemented in her later novels.

- Nearly all of Hurston's work, including her fiction, essays, and ethnographies,* describes and employs African American vernacular culture, and as such it often blends together.

- Though initially read by scholars as an accompaniment to Hurston's fiction, today "Characteristics" is seen as an important statement of the Harlem Renaissance and a step forward in the history of the study of black aesthetics.*

Positioning

Zora Neale Hurston was 39 years old when she wrote "Characteristics of Negro Expression" in 1930. Nonetheless, the essay marks a comparatively early work in her career. Hurston published several stories in the 1920s and wrote a few essays, but "Characteristics" predates all of her novels. The essay is just a small recounting of the ethnographic* material on black folklore she collected in the American South during the late 1920s—material that Hurston later expanded into *Mules and Men* (1935).

In the essay, we can observe Hurston formulating many of the ideas she would put into practice in her fiction. Every novel she later wrote would show characters speaking in black dialect,* and incorporates moments where the narration itself moves into dialect

> ❝ No matter how they read the stories Zora had
> collected, no matter how much distance they tried to
> maintain between themselves, as new sophisticates,
> and the lives their parents and grandparents lived, no
> matter how they tried to remain cool toward all Zora
> revealed, in the end they could not hold back the smiles,
> the laughter, the *joy* over who she was showing them
> to be: descendants of an inventive, joyous, courageous,
> and outrageous people: loving drama, appreciating wit,
> and, most of all, relishing the pleasure of each other's
> loquacious and *bodacious* company. ❞
>
> Alice Walker, *Zora Neale Hurston—A Cautionary Tale and A Partisan View*

speech. This is even true for her last novel, *Seraph on the Suwanee* (1948), whose main characters are white.

At the same time, "Characteristics" also responded to debates during the Harlem Renaissance, many of which took up the value of African American vernacular culture, and the political value of replicating it in art. In this sense, "Characteristics" represents an intellectual bridge between the scholarly debates of the 1920s that Hurston engaged in and the novels and non-fiction she published in the ensuing decades. Indeed, Hurston's novels themselves might be seen as forged in the crucible of these debates, responding to them decades after the participants had moved on.

Integration

It is easy to see the pieces of Hurston's artistic output as variations on a theme: demonstrating the artistic value of African American vernacular expression. Indeed, her academic work and fiction often blend into one another. While they arrive in different contexts, each borrows from the other *stylistically*—so much so that, as the English professor Michael North* notes, "it is difficult to say whether she fictionalized her ethnographic reports or whether her fiction had always been in part the product of ethnographic collecting."[1]

Hurston certainly repeated elements from different projects in her various writings. Material from *Mules and Men*, supposedly collected in 1927, appears in Hurston's fiction from before that date. *Their Eyes Were Watching God* (1937) is a *roman à clef* (a novel in which real people or events are loosely fictionalized) about Hurston's experiences growing up in Eatonville,* Florida. Indeed, Hurston's fiction is often read today for its anthropological* content, and her more anthropologically focused works for the unique viewpoint she offers within them. Much of the power of "Characteristics" lies in how Hurston generates intellectual authority. She modifies the format of the anthropological report to mirror the mode of mimicry* she describes—making the essay as much performance as description.

Hurston's first biographer Robert Hemenway describes one of Hurston's earlier works as "pure Zora Neale Hurston: part fiction, part folklore, part biography."[2] If all of Hurston's works blend these three elements—or at least put them into productive tension—then "Characteristics" represents a prime example of a work that frames this folklore through "fiction" and "biography."

Significance

Within Hurston's body of work, "Characteristics" is significantly overshadowed by her novel *Their Eyes Were Watching God* and, arguably, her book of black folklore, *Mules and Men*. In fact, scholars only began reading the essay to better understand Hurston's fiction. Thus, while the work is not superficially about fiction, it has become influential primarily as a resource for literary scholarship, and is often still encountered as such.

However, scholars have increasingly recognized the value of Hurston's essay for better understanding the debates of the Harlem Renaissance and African American aesthetics*. Part of this development is connected to Hurston's changing status in the academic world. Once considered primarily a fiction writer, Hurston is recognized today as a wide-ranging thinker, with some of her most original ideas emerging from her fictional works.

Nonetheless, the essay itself exerted little influence on Hurston's contemporaries and did not prove a game-changer in debates of the day. "Characteristics" can only be read as a crucial document of the Harlem Renaissance by focusing on its ideas. In this sense, scholars now see the essay as a powerful document that did not enjoy the prominence it deserved but nonetheless formed an important manifesto, so to speak, that Hurston followed for the rest of her writing career.

NOTES

1   Michael North, *The Dialect of Modernism: Race, Language, and Twentieth-Century Literature* (New York: Oxford University Press, 1998), 187.

2   Robert E. Hemenway, *Zora Neale Hurston: A Literary Biography* (Urbana: University of Illinois Press, 1977), 70.

SECTION 3
IMPACT

MODULE 9
THE FIRST RESPONSES

KEY POINTS

- Though we have no record of immediate responses to "Characteristics," we can hypothesize what they might have said by examining responses to Zora Neale Hurston's novels, as well as the criticisms of the essay that came later.

- While the essay itself also anticipates potential responses, these often rest on Hurston claiming personal authority about black culture.

- Although Hurston's essay remains relevant to many contemporary debates, today it is more often read as a historical document.

Criticism

While today we can see how the ideas in Zora Neale Hurston's "Characteristics of Negro Expression" influenced academic theory and African American art, we have no records of immediate response to the essay. This is largely due to its publication history: "Characteristics" was first published in Nancy Cunard's* *Negro: An Anthology* (1934), an 800-page volume that quickly went out of print and remained so until 1970.

One way to theorize potential criticism of Hurston's essay is to examine critical responses to her novel *Their Eyes Were Watching God* (1937), which implemented many of the ideas from "Characteristics." Although well received by many, the novel sparked stinging criticism from prominent black intellectuals. The author Richard Wright* famously condemned the novel for continuing "the minstrel technique that makes the 'white folks' laugh."[1] The writer and

> ❝ Miss Hurston can write, but her prose is cloaked in that facile sensuality that has dogged Negro expression since the days of Phillis Wheatley.* Her dialogue manages to catch the psychological movements of the Negro folk-mind in their pure simplicity, but that's as far as it goes. ❞
>
> Richard Wright, "Between Laughter and Tears"

educator Alain Locke* praised the novel for overcoming the stereotypes of "faulty local color fiction," but nonetheless claimed that it failed to "[dive] down deep."[2] Additionally the writer and critic Ralph Ellison* contended that the novel "retains the blight of calculated burlesque," and "was not addressed to Negro readers, but to a white audience."[3]

These critiques suggest that one potential problem with the essay lies in Hurston's glorification of rural folk culture; that by emphasizing rural dialect* speech as *most* authentically black, Hurston misses how black vernacular itself was changing as more African Americans moved to northern urban settings. It also limits the potential forms of "black art," prescribing a reenactment of southern rural speech as the *only* way an artwork can express an authentic version of "blackness."

Responses

Critics mostly writing in the 1980s and 1990s *did* offer readings of the essay. The two most prominent came from the literary and cultural critics Hazel Carby* and Paul Gilroy,* both of whom criticize Hurston for limiting the possible meanings of black expression. Carby, for example, chides Hurston for creating "a folk who are outside of history,"[4] preserving "the concept of Negroness"[5] through a utopian fantasy of an unchanging folk. Gilroy similarly admonishes Hurston's "strongly felt need to draw a line around what is and isn't authentically, genuinely, and really black."[6]

Hurston was clearly unable to respond to these criticisms from the 1980s and 1990s. We can, however, read "Characteristics" as anticipating some of these responses. While the essay reflects a staunch commitment to folk culture as the wellspring of black expression, it also takes issue with the middle-class black person who "scorns to do or be anything Negro" in an effort to "ape all the mediocrities of the white brother."[7] Hurston's response to Locke's negative review, in fact, accuses him of fitting into this category. Locke, she argued in 1938, "knows that he knows nothing about Negroes."[8]

This claim, of course, opens Hurston up to the criticism Carby and Gilroy would later offer: that her response to Locke and others asserts that she alone knows what counts as "Negro" and what doesn't.

Conflict and Consensus

As is clear from the critical responses to Hurston's fiction, Hurston and her contemporaries never reached consensus. Similarly, the larger ideas that "Characteristics" develops remain hotly contested today.

Hurston never wavered from the political and artistic commitments spelled out in her essay. Indeed, her responses to Alain Locke and Richard Wright show her doubling down on her assertion that personal history gives her special access to the folk culture that she views as most representative of African American-ness. The novels that followed Hurston's essay—*Jonah's Gourd Vine* (1934), *Their Eyes Were Watching God* (1937), *Moses, Man of the Mountain* (1939), and *Seraph on the Suwanee* (1948)—all focus on vernacular expression as essential to the endurance of black culture. Thus, while some ideas in Hurston's essay still maintain potential relevance for contemporary debates about "authenticity"* and black expression, the essay now tends to be read as a historical document that crystalizes an earlier moment in black aesthetic theory.* And rather than argue about whether Hurston properly conveyed the nature of black expression, critics today focus more on Hurston's claim that she alone could do so.

NOTES

1   Richard Wright, "Between Laughter and Tears," *New Masses* 25 (1937): 22–5.

2   Alain Locke, "Review of *Their Eyes Were Watching God*," *Opportunity* (1938).

3   Ralph Ellison, "Recent Negro Fiction," *New Masses* 40, no. 6 (1941): 22–6.

4   Hazel V. Carby, "The Politics of Fiction, Anthropology, and the Folk: Zora Neale Hurston," in *New Essays on Their Eyes Were Watching God*, ed. Michael Awkward (Cambridge: Cambridge University Press, 1991);77.

5   Carby, "The Politics of Fiction," 79.

6   Paul Gilroy, *The Black Atlantic: Modernity and Double-Consciousness* (Cambridge, MA: Harvard University Press, 1993),

7   Zora Neale Hurston, "Characteristics of Negro Expression," in *Within the Circle: An Anthology of African American Literary Criticism From the Harlem Renaissance to the Present*, ed. Angelyn Mitchell (Durham, NC: Duke University Press, 1994), 87.

8   Zora Neale Hurston, "The Chick With One Hen.Typescript Carbon Corrected," Box 1, Folder 8a, Zora Neale Hurston Collection, Beinecke Rare Book & Manuscript Library, Yale University.

MODULE 10
THE EVOLVING DEBATE

KEY POINTS

- Many thinkers have developed Hurston's description of African American art as more about process than content, as well as her claims about the authenticity of vernacular* speech.

- Both the Black Arts Movement* of the 1960s and 1970s and the novels of the writers Toni Morrison* and Alice Walker* provide examples of art that views vernacular expression as the source of authenticity.

- Over the last 30 years, the two major theories of African American expression, from the cultural and literary critics Henry Louis Gates, Jr.* and Houston Baker,* have both extended Hurston's account of mimicry.*

Uses and Problems

While the idea that African American artistry is more about process than content (that is, we must look to the method to find meaning) certainly predates Zora Neale Hurston's "Characteristics of Negro Expression," the essay encapsulates it in a way that has inspired many scholars of black aesthetics.* Arguably the most influential of Hurston's claims concerns the hymns known as Negro spirituals;* as she writes in "Spirituals and Neo-Spirituals" that a spiritual is not "a final thing"[1] but a loose form that generates a new and different version of itself with each performance.

For example, Amiri Baraka,* the poet and founder of the Black Arts Movement,* famously described African American cultural expression with the term "the changing same."[2] This phrase captures the way black art forms such as jazz and storytelling repeatedly utilize

> **❝** As far as I'm concerned, she is my aunt—and that of all black people as well. **❞**
>
> Alice Walker, "Looking for Zora"

the same forms, with the artist expressing him or herself in the unique way he or she performs those songs or stories. The American scholar James Snead* further develops this idea in his seminal essay "Repetition as a Figure of Black Culture" (1984), which discusses the role of "progress within cycle, 'differentiation' within repetition"[3] in black artistry. More recently, the poet and critic Fred Moten's* book *In the Break* (2003) pushed this idea into a more poststructuralist* direction.[4] ("Poststructuralism" refers to a set of philosophical theories often concerned with pointing out the instability of theoretical systems and the role of language in the construction of meaning.)

Hurston's contention that vernacular* speech more authentically represents the African American world view has also animated many artistic movements. The debates to which "Characteristics" responded are still carried out today in discussions about hip-hop* music. While artists often claim that their language depicts the experiences of their communities (the political rapper Chuck D* famously called rap "the black CNN"[5]), critics such as the comedian Bill Cosby have accused hip-hop of reinforcing stereotypes.

Schools of Thought

The ideas in "Characteristics" have reappeared in many African American artistic movements, most notably the Black Arts Movement of the 1960s, that called for reclaiming black vernacular language and developing literary forms attuned to it. We can hear Hurston's words echo in the statements of the writer and scholar Larry Neal,* another architect of the movement. He argued that "we can learn more about what poetry is by listening to the cadences in Malcolm [X]'s* speeches, than from most of Western poetics. Listen to James Brown* scream."[6] Similarly, Neal's call for "literature as a *living* reality"[7] echoes Hurston's claim that authentic black culture cannot be found in static performances of Negro spirituals by the Fisk Jubilee Singers* vocal group.

Hurston's work has also indelibly shaped African American fiction. Toni Morrison's novel *Song of Solomon* (1977) provides a near case study of Hurston's ideas. Its main character, Macon Dead, begins as a northern black man alienated from himself and his culture, but reconnects with his identity by travelling to the South, where he realizes that black vernacular speech connects him to a time "before language. Before things were written down."[8]

The writer Alice Walker played a crucial role in reviving interest in Hurston's work and cites Hurston as a major influence. One can see this in Walker's novel *The Color Purple* (1982), which narrates its main character's growing ability to express herself in her own language.

In Current Scholarship

Many African American literary critics have developed theories that utilize Hurston's work. Perhaps the most influential theory of African American expression in the last 30 years is Henry Louis Gates Jr.'s theory of "signifyin(g),"[9] developed in his work *The Signifying Monkey* (1988). In this context, signifyin(g) indicates the process whereby black speakers add meanings to standard English words, so that those words register on two levels of meaning: using the word "cool" to mean "good" would be a very basic example. In other words, "signifyin(g)" is a kind of mimicry. Gates devotes a whole chapter of his book to Hurston's novel *Their Eyes Were Watching God*, which he believes offers the first instance of what he calls a *speakerly* text: a "text whose rhetorical strategy is designed to present an oral literary tradition."[10]

The other major theorist of African American expression has been Houston Baker* who, in his book *Modernism and the Harlem Renaissance*,* develops a theory he describes with the terms "mastery of form" and "deformation of mastery."[11] "Mastery of form" refers to the ability to mimic stereotypical representations of African American identity in order to hide behind them and create a space of safety. "Deformation of mastery" indicates an artist's modifying a set of artistic forms to *refuse* these stereotypes. Though Baker does not reference Hurston in his theory, these processes also work as a kind of mimicry—artistically modifying a received cultural allusion to produce a new result.

NOTES

1   Zora Neale Hurston, "Spirituals and Neo-Spirituals," in *Negro: An Anthology*, ed. Nancy Cunard (New York: Continuum, 1996).

2   LeRoi Jones (Amiri Baraka), "The Changing Same (R&B and New Black Music)," in *Black Music* (New York: William Morrow, 1970).

3   James A. Snead, "Repetition as a Figure of Black Culture," in *Black Literature and Literary Theory*, ed. Henry Louis Gates, Jr. (New York: Methuen, 1984), 65.

4   Fred Moten, *In the Break: The Aesthetics of the Black Radical Tradition* (Minneapolis: University of Minnesota Press, 2003).

5   Chuck D with Yusuf Jah, *Fight the Power: Rap, Race, and Reality* (New York: Delacorte Press, 1997), 256.

6   Larry Neal, "And Shine Swam on," in *Black Fire: An Anthology of Afro-American Writing*, ed. LeRoi Jones (Amiri Baraka) and Larry Neal (Baltimore: Black Classic Press, 2007), 653.

7   Neal, "And Shine Swam on," 654.

8   Toni Morrison, *Song of Solomon* (New York: Alfred A. Knopf, Inc., 1977), 281.

9   Henry Louis Gates, Jr., *The Signifying Monkey: A Theory of African-American Literary Criticism* (New York: Oxford University Press, 1988).

10 Gates, *The Signifying Monkey*, 181.

11 Houston A. Baker, *Modernism and the Harlem Renaissance* (Chicago: University of Chicago Press, 1987), 15.

MODULE 11
IMPACT AND INFLUENCE TODAY

KEY POINTS

- Today, "Characteristics" is seen as a crucial text for understanding Zora Neale Hurston's fiction, for clarifying debates about the Harlem Renaissance,* and helping trace the history of African American aesthetic* criticism.

- The ideas in the essay remain strikingly relevant to developments in art today, particularly those around "authenticity"* and "authority."

- Numerous African American artists and intellectuals have questioned the essay's claims about authenticity, arguing that these claims hamper creative possibilities.

Position

With every decade since the 1970s, the number of critical works engaging with Zora Neale Hurston's "Characteristics of Negro Expression" has grown significantly. Its progressive inclusion in anthologies of African American criticism—and the expanding contexts in which it is employed—reflect the essay's importance. The text has also become crucial for understanding the intellectual debates of the Harlem Renaissance, as a valuable resource for analyzing Hurston's fiction, and as an important signpost in the history of black aesthetic theory.*

Eighty years have passed since Hurston's essay was published, and changes in American culture have rendered some of her ideas more anachronistic than others. Her theory that American culture is formed from a give-and-take between different groups is now less provocative and more widely accepted. Indeed, hip-hop* is popular among

> **❝** Hurston is now a cardinal figure in the Afro-
> American canon, the feminist canon, and the canon of
> American fiction. **❞**
>
> Henry Louis Gates, Jr., *The Signifying Monkey: A Theory of African-American Literary Criticism*

suburban white youth, and American slang comes predominantly
from black culture. Many black artists today—from the conceptual
artist Glenn Ligon* to the filmmaker Justin Simien*—make art
whose authenticity comes from the way it questions the expectations
that it be traditionally "black," rather than how it fits criteria that
Hurston describes.

Nonetheless, "Characteristics," while not yet considered a classic
on the level of Hurston's best fiction, still challenges readers with its
premise that for them to understand African American art, they must
understand the values of the culture in which it originates.

Interaction

Though more commonly read from a historical perspective, the essay
might surprise new readers, given how its ideas anticipate many
contemporary debates about authentic African American art. For
example, a common criticism of contemporary white pop-music
artists is that they try to "sound black." The list of these artists stretches
from the singer Elvis Presley* to the British rock group the Rolling
Stones* and white US rappers the Beastie Boys,* to more recent
artists such as white rappers Eminem,* Iggy Azalea,* and
Macklemore.*

The criticism almost directly mirrors Hurston's claim that white
artists such as jazz composer George Gershwin* and dancer Ann
Pennington* "have all the elements," but that those elements are
"displaced or distorted."[1] The implication is often that these artists

borrow from black culture without understanding it or participating in the experiences that gave rise to it—without having, in Hurston's words, "[lived] and [moved] in the midst of a white civilization"[2] that is antagonistic to who one is.

These criticisms also speak to a key question raised in "Characteristics": who has the authority to decide what authentic African American expression is? Hurston's essay emphatically declares the answer to be Hurston herself—and arguably Hurston alone. But this discussion still plays out on a near-daily basis in magazines, on the web, on talk shows, in comment pieces, and in the news. These questions have become more prominent in the twenty-first century, given the election in 2008 of an African American of mixed ancestry, Barak Obama,* to the position of president of the United States. His simple presence in the White House has spurred prominent debates about what counts as authentically "black," and who gets to decide.

The Continuing Debate

While few writers responded directly to "Characteristics," many African American intellectuals have criticized what they see as the authoritative and restrictive implications of some of its key ideas.

Perhaps most problematic has been Hurston's implicit claim that authentic African American expression is found only in folk and vernacular* culture. Many artists have since argued that that this creates an inescapable bind. To express what they want to express, such artists might not find black vernacular language appropriate. But if their art does *not* conform to vernacular forms, they argue, it is often dismissed as "not black enough." The writer Percival Everett,* for example, parodies this problem in his satirical novel *Erasure* (2001), which suggests that "authentic" black vernacular may not be as easy to identify as Hurston believes. Everett's protagonist—an educated, black English professor who writes experimental modernist fiction—spitefully writes an anonymous parody of the "ghetto novel" genre called *My Pafology*, only to see it hailed as a masterpiece: "honest, so raw, so down-and-dirty-gritty, so real."[3] In the academic world, the critic Kenneth Warren* recently provoked debate with his book *What Was African American Literature?* (2011), which argues that black literature should not be understood as an ongoing project but as a particular historical event generated in response to the Jim Crow* laws (a set of laws operating between 1890 and 1965 that enforced racial segregation). Read within Warren's account, Hurston's work would be important only for making a political argument against the alleged inferiority of African Americans—but not for having captured anything essential about African American identity.

As the very meaning of "African American" expands and changes, Hurston's essay remains a thought-provoking lens through which to watch these dynamics unfold.

NOTES

1   Zora Neale Hurston, "Characteristics of Negro Expression," in *Within the Circle: An Anthology of African American Literary Criticism From the Harlem Renaissance to the Present*, ed. Angelyn Mitchell (Durham, NC: Duke University Press, 1994), 92.

2   Hurston, "Characteristics of Negro Expression," 86.

3   Percival Everett, *Erasure* (New York: Hyperion, 2001), 260.

MODULE 12
WHERE NEXT?

KEY POINTS

- While not often considered the foundational text of any particular discipline, "Characteristics" remains useful for both historical research and understanding black vernacular* culture today.

- "Characteristics" still offers a powerful theory of black creative expression, carried forward in both academic and literary settings.

- Questions about African American experience have become perhaps more prominent today, which makes Hurston's essay an especially valuable resource.

Potential

Despite offering a powerful, provocative model for understanding African American art and culture, Zora Neale Hurston's "Characteristics of Negro Expression" is still not the first place most people go to learn about the Harlem Renaissance,* African American aesthetics,* black folklore, or even Hurston's own work. More often the essay works as a supplement to all these: a puzzle piece that fits many historical and theoretical contexts.

Yet while some of the essay's arguments seem outmoded today—the claim that "the white man thinks in a written language and the Negro thinks in hieroglyphics,"[1] for example—its contributions to many larger cultural debates remain as relevant as they were a century ago. Though the isolated, rural African American culture Hurston turned to for her ethnographic* analyses has largely disappeared, black vernacular art still flourishes. "Urban fiction" or "street lit," for

> **❝** Serena and her big sister Venus Williams brought to mind Zora Neale Hurston's 'I feel most colored when I am thrown against a sharp white background.' **❞**
>
> Claudia Rankine, *Citizen: An American Lyric*

example, remains a literature written and consumed by an almost exclusively African American audience; it is still largely sold on street-corner stands in New York and other cities, or on the Internet, as self-published work. On the other side of the spectrum sit artists who argue that the African American experience is today too divergent, localized, or diffuse for any one mode of speech or expression.

To both of these groups, "Characteristics" offers an argument whose larger contours still outline the major debates about African American identity and expression. Though less cited than it could be, the essay remains important not only for scholars interested in African American history, but also for informing larger debates about identity and performance.

Future Directions

In an essay on Hurston, the writer Alice Walker* identifies the most important quality of Hurston's body of work as "racial health—a sense of black people as complete, complex, *undiminished* human beings."[2] The ongoing quest to capture the complexity of African American identity—and to value that experience as one that still shapes American culture as a whole—continues to animate literary and academic projects. Academic theorists such as Fred Moten* extend the legacy; his *In the Break: The Aesthetics of the Black Radical Tradition* (2003) outlines a poststructuralist* black aesthetics. Similarly, the poet Kevin Young's* *The Grey Album: On the Blackness of Blackness* (2012) echoes Hurston in its blend of academic analysis and literary experimentation.

In the literary field, many African American writers carry on Hurston's project of capturing the "authentic" vernacular voice—or charting the complexities, if not impossibility, of such an endeavor. The poet Claudia Rankine's* *Citizen: An American Lyric* (2014) perhaps represents the most powerful of these works. While she refuses to define a true African American identity (as Hurston has been accused of doing), her book nonetheless provides a deep vision of how outside experiences structure a unique African American perspective. Evie Shockley's* book of poetry *The New Black* (2011) rethinks traditional poetic forms to explore black identity; fiction writers such as Colson Whitehead* write about the difficulties of maintaining ties to "authentic black culture" in upper-class contexts; and satirists including Paul Beatty* have skewered the expectations placed on black writers.

While these various writers may not cite "Characteristics" directly, one can easily see all of them extending Hurston's project on the multiple levels where it works: the academic, the literary, *and* the personal.

Summary

Zora Neale Hurston's essay stands as a seminal text of twentieth-century African American literature. It presents an aesthetic theory of black expression that portrays the features of black art as singular and innovative. "Characteristics" concentrates on form rather than content, and the original, unique modes of expression black people employ. Most importantly, it provides a new framework for understanding why African American art works the way it does, citing examples drawn from many areas of black cultural life.

Those reading the essay today are likely to see its immediate relevance to contemporary society. In a time when many characterize contemporary society as "post-racial"—that is, in which racial matters are no longer as urgent—it is increasingly important to think about the ways that racial categories play a large role in shaping a person's identity and experience. Given this, the essay's implicit premise still holds relevance today: that to understand the aesthetics of a given culture, those aesthetics must be evaluated based on the goals *of that culture*.

In addition, the essay also argues for a notion of American society itself as an exchange of cultural practices between groups. While Hurston was primarily concerned with the exchange between African American and white cultures, American society in the twenty-first century only opens new contexts for a Hurston-inspired analysis of increasing sociocultural diversity—and how that impacts art and culture.

At a time when "appropriation"* (the copying by a dominant cultural group of cultural elements produced by a minority) has become a hot-button term in American culture, when people debate the ethics of the African American dance form known as "twerking,"* when racial classifications become ever more blurred scientifically yet more deeply entrenched culturally (particularly around law enforcement's stance towards African Americans), Hurston's essay provides a framework that clarifies these issues. With the rise of the "Black Lives Matter"* movement in America, raising awareness of systematic violence against black Americans, the nature of African American experience has received long-awaited cultural attention.

Hurston, who died in poverty in 1960 with her work relegated to obscurity, would no doubt take heart to see the reputation her essay enjoys more than 80 years after its publication. For its originality in interpreting and embodying what makes African American art vital, Zora Neale Hurston's "Characteristics of Negro Expression" remains a critical touchstone.

NOTES

1   Zora Neale Hurston, "Characteristics of Negro Expression," in *Within the Circle: An Anthology of African American Literary Criticism From the Harlem Renaissance to the Present*, ed. Angelyn Mitchell (Durham, NC: Duke University Press, 1994), 80.

2   Alice Walker, "Zora Neale Hurston—a Cautionary Tale and a Partisan View," in *In Search of Our Mothers' Gardens* (New York: Harcourt Brace Jovanovich, 1984), 83.

GLOSSARY

GLOSSARY OF TERMS

Aesthetics/Aesthetic theory: the philosophy of the beautiful, or the philosophy of art. Aesthetic theory attempts to determine what art is, how it works, and what it means.

Anthropology: the study of human beings, particularly their cultures, societies, language, and biology.

Appropriation: a cultural process in which a dominant group copies cultural elements taken from a minority group. These copied elements are often used outside their original context. Appropriation is considered disrespectful by many critics, although this claim has been the subject of much debate.

Authenticity: the degree to which an artwork or cultural practice can be said to represent the authentic nature of the culture from which it comes.

Baptist Church: a Christian denomination that emphasizes the importance of the Christian sacrament of baptism.

Black Arts Movement: a movement, started by the poet Amiri Baraka (then LeRoi Jones) in 1965, self-described as the "aesthetic and spiritual sister of the Black Power movement." Artists in the movement strove to make art that was actively political, both in capturing the essence of the African American experience and pushing for African American independence in businesses and art institutions.

Blackface: a style of exaggerated American comedy in which white actors would wear black make-up and perform caricatured representations of black people. Blackface theater was popular in the

United States in the nineteenth century and the first half of the twentieth.

Black Lives Matter: an American activist movement aimed at raising awareness of violence against African Americans. Begun in 2013, the movement has grown in the wake of the publicized killings of unarmed African American men by police officers.

Dialect literature: a style of fiction that attempts to capture the style of speaking particular to a specific geographical region. In American literature, writing in dialect has been one of the ways by which writers distinguished their writing as "American" as opposed to "European."

Double consciousness: a theory of African American identity described by the social theorist W. E. B. Du Bois in his book *The Souls of Black Folk* (1903). Double consciousness theorizes that African Americans hold two versions of self-identity, as both "American" and "Negro," and that, because of America's scorn for the Negro, the African American is therefore in permanent conflict with himself. Du Bois's theory has proved to be one of the most influential theories in African American studies over the last century.

Eatonville, Florida: a city in the southern United States. Incorporated in 1887, Eatonville was one of the first American municipalities started and governed exclusively by African Americans.

Essentialism: the belief that entities, particular different types of people (men, women, people of specific ethnicities), possess unchanging features that define what it is to be the specific kind of people they are. Essentialism is often opposed to "constructivism," which is the belief that these identities are the result of social structures and norms.

Ethnography: the research and presentation of empirical data on a human culture. Ethnography attempts to describe the various social phenomena of a group, using data gathered firsthand by the researcher.

Fisk Jubilee Singers: an African American vocal group, originally organized in 1871 at Fisk University, whose repertoire generally consists of Negro spirituals. The group has performed to audiences throughout the world and continues to tour and record.

Folklorist: a person who studies the traditional beliefs, myths, tales, and practices of a people that are transmitted orally. Hurston collected stories as a folklorist for "Characteristics of Negro Expression."

Harlem: a neighborhood in the northern section of the borough of Manhattan, in New York City. From 1905 on, the neighborhood's demographics became increasingly African American, and for many years was a central location of African American culture.

Harlem Renaissance: an artistic and social movement that took place in the 1920s and 1930s, largely in the neighborhood of Harlem in New York City. Encompassing literature, music, dance, visual art, and philosophy, the movement was the largest and most focused flowering of African American art and culture up to that point.

Hip-hop: a cultural movement started in New York City in the 1970s, primarily by young African American men and women. While the term "hip-hop" is meant to encompass rap music, graffiti, break-dancing, and deejaying, today the word is most often associated with rap music and its accompanying culture.

Incorporated town: a town with a charter received from the state similar to a city that has elected officials. Eatonville, Florida, where

Hurston grew up, was one of the first black incorporated towns in the US.

Jim Crow: a set of laws that maintained racial segregation in the United States. These laws, which mandated separate schools, public places, drinking fountains, and many more instances of segregation, lasted from 1890 to 1965, but in practice took longer to eradicate.

Mimicry: the act of imitating some aspect of art or language and altering it to create something new. In Hurston's essay, mimicry applies not only to traditional arts such as poetry, painting, and music, but also to any area of life where African Americans express themselves: religion, slang, folklore, home decorating, and more.

Minstrel show: an American entertainment form, popular in the nineteenth and early twentieth centuries, in which white performers in blackface, or later black performers, performed skits and musical numbers in ways that caricatured black people.

Opportunity: a journal founded in 1923 and run by African American sociologist and activist Charles S. Johnson (1893–1956) in New York City. *Opportunity* was one of the most important journals of the Harlem Renaissance, publishing groundbreaking literary works and sponsoring literary contests.

Phrenology: a discredited scientific method, common from the late eighteenth century through the early twentieth, that believed that measuring the human skull could reveal a person's innate intelligence or moral character.

Poststructuralism: a set of philosophical theories that emerged in the 1960s in France, Continental Europe, and the United States. Often concerned with pointing out the instability of theoretical systems and the role of language in the construction of meaning, poststructuralism is most associated with figures such as Jacques Derrida, Michel Foucault, and Jacques Lacan.

Scientific racism: the use of scientific techniques, often debatable, to validate the belief that certain racial groups are inherently superior or inferior to others.

Spirituals: a set of religious songs created by American slaves. Spirituals generally mixed Christian hymns with African musical and performance styles, and combined images of freedom and heaven to describe the hopes of slaves.

Tuskegee Choir: a singing group founded in 1881 at Tuskegee University, an African American university in Alabama. Like the Fisk Jubilee Singers, the Tuskegee Choir has travelled the world, performing Negro spirituals to wide acclaim.

Twerking: a style of dancing that originated in the African American community, but became controversial when Miley Cyrus, a white singer, performed it in public in 2013.

Uncle Tom: a derogatory term for an African American person seen as acting in a servile manner towards white people, often to improve his own economic or social situation. Although the phrase comes from Harriet Beecher Stowe's novel *Uncle Tom's Cabin* (1852), Stowe's character Uncle Tom does not generally exhibit these behaviors.

Vernacular: the native or dialect language of a specific region. Vernacular often designates informal spoken language or slang, as opposed to more proper or formal written language.

PEOPLE MENTIONED IN THE TEXT

Iggy Azalea (b. 1990) is a white Australian rapper who raps in a southern American accent. Her song "Fancy" reached number one on the US Billboard Hot 100 chart in 2014.

Houston Baker (b. 1943) is an American literary critic, currently teaching at Vanderbilt University. He is best known for his theories of African American literature.

Amiri Baraka (1934–2014), born Everett LeRoi Jones, was an American poet, critic, activist, and playwright. One of the most influential and controversial African American writers of the postwar period, he founded the Black Arts Repertory/Theater School in 1965, giving birth to the Black Arts Movement.

The Beastie Boys were an American hip-hop group, founded in New York City in 1981. Their albums include *Paul's Boutique*, *License to Ill*, *Check Your Head*, *Ill Communication* and *Hello Nasty*.

Paul Beatty (b. 1962) is an African American author and humorist. His books include *The White Boy Shuffle* (1996) and *The Sellout* (2015).

Franz Boas (1858–1942) was a German American anthropologist often called the "Father of American Anthropology." He is famous for arguing that cultures cannot be compared along any objective axis, a position now called "cultural relativism."

Roark Bradford (1896–1948) was an American fiction writer famous for his dialect literature.

William Stanley Braithwaite (1878–1962) was an African American writer and literary critic. From 1913 to 1929, Braithwaite published the *Anthology of Magazine Verse*, a yearly poetry anthology that introduced many famous Harlem Renaissance writers.

James Brown (1933–2006) was an African American musician credited with inventing funk music. He was often called "The Godfather of Soul."

Hazel Carby (b. 1948) is a literary critic, currently teaching at Yale University. She is known for her work on African American literature, gender, and feminism, and postcolonialism.

Chuck D (b. 1960) is an American rapper, noted for leading the hip-hop group Public Enemy.

Octavus Roy Cohen (1891–1959) was a white American author who wrote many books containing black characters speaking in egregiously exaggerated dialect.

Countee Cullen (1903–46) was an American poet and fiction writer. He is considered one of the most important poets of the Harlem Renaissance. **Nancy Cunard (1896–1965)** was a British writer and activist. In 1934 she published *Negro: An Anthology*, which included Zora Neale Hurston's essay "Characteristics of Negro Expression," among others.

Frederick Douglass (1818–95) was a writer, orator, and ex-slave who became a leader of the abolitionist movement. He was one of the most famous African Americans of the nineteenth century, and is considered one of the most influential African American writers of the past 200 years.

W. E. B. Du Bois (1868–1963) was an African American writer, philosopher, sociologist, activist, and historian. He was a prominent American intellectual for many years, a co-founder of the National Association for the Advancement of Colored People (NAACP), and wrote many books, including *The Souls of Black Folk* (1903).

Ralph Ellison (1914–94) was an American writer and critic. He wrote the novel *Invisible Man* (1952).

Eminem (b. Marshall Bruce Mathers III, 1972) is an American rapper and record producer. Though white, he is often considered one of the best rappers in the hip-hop tradition.

Percival Everett (b. 1956) is an American novelist and short-story writer. He is the recipient of many literary awards, and currently teaches at the University of Southern California.

Henry Louis Gates, Jr. (b. 1950) is an American literary critic and filmmaker who currently teaches at Harvard University. He is considered one of the country's foremost African American intellectuals, and has written many books, including *The Signifying Monkey* (1988), an influential book of African American literary criticism.

George Gershwin (1898–1937) was an American composer famous for blending jazz and classical influences, and writing both classical and popular music. His works include *Rhapsody in Blue* and the opera *Porgy and Bess*.

Paul Gilroy (b. 1956) is a British cultural and literary critic, currently teaching at King's College London. His book *The Black Atlantic: Modernity and Double Consciousness* (1993) is considered a seminal work in diaspora studies.

Langston Hughes (1902–67) was an African American poet. He is known for being a leading figure in the Harlem Renaissance, and for being one of the twentieth century's most important American poets.

George Hutchinson is the Newton C. Farr professor of American culture at Cornell University. His book *The Harlem Renaissance in Black and White* (1995) is considered one of the crucial critical studies of the period.

Al Jolson (1886–1950) was a singer, actor, and comedian, one of America's most famous entertainers in the first part of the twentieth century. He often sang jazz and blues music, and often performed in blackface.

Glenn Ligon (b. 1960) is an American artist whose work often engages issues of race and identity.

Alain Locke (1885–1954) was an African American writer and educator. He spent most of his career as a professor at Howard University, and is known for publishing *The New Negro* (1925), a collection of African American writing that is considered one of the critical works of the Harlem Renaissance.

Alan Lomax (1915–2002) was an American folklorist and ethnomusicologist. He is famous for the thousands of field recordings he made of folk and blues musicians in the late 1930s.

Macklemore (b. Ben Haggerty, 1983) is a white American rapper. In 2014, Macklemore won a Grammy Award for Best Rap Album, a controversial result, given that the black rapper Kendrick Lamar's album from the same year generally received far more praise from the critics.

Claude McKay (1889–1948) was a Jamaican American writer. He is considered an important member of the Harlem Renaissance, and wrote many poems and books, including the novels *Home to Harlem* (1928) and *Banjo* (1929).

Toni Morrison (b. 1931) is a Nobel Prize-winning novelist. She has published many acclaimed novels, including *The Bluest Eye* (1970), *Sula* (1973), *Song of Solomon* (1977), and *Beloved* (1987), which won the Pulitzer Prize.

Fred Moten (b. 1962) is an American poet, literary critic, and cultural theorist, currently teaching at the University of California, Riverside. His 2003 book *In the Break: The Aesthetics of the Black Radical Tradition* has become one of the most influential books in contemporary African American aesthetic thought.

Larry Neal (1937–81) was an African American writer and scholar. Along with Amiri Baraka, he is considered one of the founders of the Black Arts Movement.

Michael North is a professor in the department of English at UCLA. His work focuses on modernism, race, literature, and visual art.

Barak Obama (b. 1961) is the 44th president of the United States.

Ann Pennington (1893–1971) was an American dancer and performer. In the 1920s she became famous for popularizing a dance called the "Black Bottom."

Elvis Presley (1935–77) was an American singer known as the "The King." He is considered one of the first major rock-and-roll singers in America, and often adapted black musical styles in his music.

Claudia Rankine (b. 1963) is a Jamaican poet, currently teaching at the University of Southern California. Her works include *Don't Let Me Be Lonely* (2004) and *Citizen: An American Lyric* (2014), which won the National Book Critics Circle award for poetry.

The Rolling Stones are an English rock band, founded in 1962. They are famous for incorporating American blues music into their songs.

George Schuyler (1895–1977) was an African American author. He is considered one of the more politically conservative members of the Harlem Renaissance, and his book *Black No More* (1931) is considered an early example of black science fiction.

Evie Shockley (b. 1965) is a poet and academic, currently teaching at Rutgers University.

Justin Simien (b. 1983) is an American filmmaker. His film *Dear White People* was released in 2014.

James Snead (1953–89) was an African American academic who taught at Yale and the University of Pittsburgh.

Herbert Spencer (1820–1903) was a British scientist and philosopher. He is famous for coining the phrase "survival of the fittest" to describe the principle of evolution.

Alice Walker (b. 1944) is an African American writer and activist. She is most famous for her novel *The Color Purple* (1982), which won the Pulitzer Prize and was made into a well-known film.

Kenneth Warren is a literary critic, currently teaching at the University of Chicago. His work focuses on African American literature, particularly African American novels and their relationship to social change.

Ethel Waters (1896–1977) was an American singer and actress. Known as a member of the Harlem Renaissance, she recorded many famous versions of popular jazz and blues songs.

Mae West (1893–1980) was an American singer and actress. She was famous for her highly sexualized persona.

Phillis Wheatley (1753–84) was the first African American female poet to be published in the United States. Born in Africa, she became a slave at the age of eight and was later legally freed.

Colson Whitehead (b. 1969) is an American novelist. His books include *The Intuitionist* (1999), *John Henry Days* (2001), *Sag Harbor* (2009), and *Zone One* (2011).

Paul Whiteman (1890–1967) was a white American bandleader. He became popular in the 1920s, and was known briefly as the "King of Jazz," although he was also accused of appropriating an African American musical form.

Richard Wright (1908–60) was an African American novelist and essayist. He was known as a social realist, and is most famous for his novels *Native Son* (1940) and *Black Boy* (1945).

Malcolm X (1925–65) was an African American activist and a Muslim minister. He is widely considered one of the most important African American political leaders of the postwar period.

Kevin Young (b. 1970) is an American poet, currently teaching at Emory University. His works include *To Repel Ghosts* (2002), *Jelly Roll* (2005), and *Black Maria* (2005).

WORKS CITED

WORKS CITED

Allen, William Francis, Charles Pickard Ware, and Lucy McKim Garrison, eds. *Slave Songs of the United States*. New York: Peter Smith, 1867.

Baker, Houston A. *Modernism and the Harlem Renaissance*. Chicago: University of Chicago Press, 1987.

Boyd, Valerie. *Wrapped in Rainbows: The Life of Zora Neale Hurston*. New York: Scribner, 2003.

Carby, Hazel V. "The Politics of Fiction, Anthropology, and the Folk: Zora Neale Hurston." In *New Essays on Their Eyes Were Watching God*, edited by Michael Awkward, 71–94. Cambridge: Cambridge University Press, 1991.

D, Chuck with Yusuf Jah. *Fight the Power: Rap, Race, and Reality*. New York: Delacorte Press, 1997.

Douglass, Frederick. *Narrative of the Life of Frederick Douglass, an American Slave*. Edited by John W. Blassingame, John R. McKivigan, and Peter P. Hinks. New Haven, CT: Yale University Press, 2001.

Du Bois, W. E. B. "Criteria of Negro Art." In *The Portable Harlem Renaissance Reader*, edited by David Levering Lewis, 100–5. New York: Viking Penguin, 1994.

The Souls of Black Folk. New York: Penguin Books, 1996.

Ellison, Ralph. "Recent Negro Fiction." *New Masses* 40, no. 6 (1941): 22–6.

Everett, Percival. *Erasure*. New York: Hyperion, 2001.

Gates, Henry Louis, Jr. *The Signifying Monkey: A Theory of African-American Literary Criticism*. New York: Oxford University Press, 1988.

Gilroy, Paul. *The Black Atlantic: Modernity and Double-Consciousness*. Cambridge, MA: Harvard University Press, 1993.

Hemenway, Robert E. *Zora Neale Hurston: A Literary Biography*. Urbana: University of Illinois Press, 1977.

Hughes, Langston. "The Negro Artist and the Racial Mountain." In *The Portable Harlem Renaissance Reader*, edited by David Levering Lewis, 91–5. New York: Viking Penguin, 1994.

Hurston, Zora Neale. *Mules and Men*. New York: HarperPerennial, 1935.

Dust Tracks on a Road. New York: HarperPerennial, 1942.

"Characteristics of Negro Expression." In *Within the Circle: An Anthology of African American Literary Criticism From the Harlem Renaissance to the Present*, edited by Angelyn Mitchell, 79–94. Durham, NC: Duke University Press, 1994.

"Spirituals and Neo-Spirituals." In *Negro: An Anthology*, edited by Nancy Cunard, 223–5. New York: Continuum, 1996.

"The Chick With One Hen.Typescript Carbon Corrected." Box 1, Folder 8a, Zora Neale Hurston Collection. Beinecke Rare Book & Manuscript Library, Yale University.

Hutchinson, George. *The Harlem Renaissance in Black and White*. Cambridge, MA: Harvard University Press, 1995.

Jacobs, Karen. *The Eye's Mind: Literary Modernism and Visual Culture*. Ithaca, NY: Cornell University Press, 2001.

Jones, LeRoi (Amiri Baraka). "The Changing Same (R&B and New Black Music)." In *Black Music*, 180–211. New York: William Morrow, 1970.

Locke, Alain. "Enter the New Negro." *The Survey Graphic* VI, no. 6 (1925): 631–34.

"Review of Their Eyes Were Watching God." *Opportunity* (1938):

"Art Or Propaganda?" In *Voices of the Harlem Renaissance*, edited by Nathan Irvin Huggins, 312–13. New York: Oxford University Press, 1976.

"The New Negro." In *The Portable Harlem Renaissance Reader*, edited by David Levering Lewis, 46–51. New York: Viking Penguin, 1994.

Morrison, Toni. *Song of Solomon*. New York: Alfred A. Knopf, 1977.

Moten, Fred. *In the Break: The Aesthetics of the Black Radical Tradition*. Minneapolis: University of Minnesota Press, 2003.

Neal, Larry. "And Shine Swam on." In *Black Fire: An Anthology of Afro-American Writing*, edited by LeRoi Jones (Amiri Baraka) and Larry Neal, 637–56. Baltimore: Black Classic Press, 2007.

North, Michael. *The Dialect of Modernism: Race, Language, and Twentieth-Century Literature*. New York: Oxford University Press, 1998.

Pilgrim, David. "The Coon Caricature." Jim Crow Museum of Racist Memorabilia (2012). Accessed November 25, 2015. http://www.ferris.edu/news/jimcrow/coon/.

Rankine, Claudia. *Citizen: An American Lyric*. Minneapolis: Graywolf Press, 2014.

Schuyler, George. "The Negro-Art Hokum." In *The Portable Harlem Renaissance Reader*, edited by David Levering Lewis, 96–9. New York: Viking Penguin, 1994.

Snead, James A. "Repetition as a Figure of Black Culture." In *Black Literature and Literary Theory*, edited by Henry Louis Gates, Jr., New York: Methuen, 1984.

Walker, Alice. "Looking for Zora." In *In Search of Our Mothers' Gardens*, 93–116. New York: Harcourt Brace Jovanovich, 1984.

"Zora Neale Hurston—a Cautionary Tale and a Partisan View." In *In Search of Our Mothers' Gardens*, 83–92. New York: Harcourt Brace Jovanovich, 1984.

Wall, Cheryl A. "Zora Neale Hurston's Essays: On Art and Such." *S&F Online* 3, no. 2 (2005). Accessed November 25, 2015. http://sfonline.barnard.edu/hurston/wall_01.htm.

Warren, Kenneth W. *What Was African American Literature?* Cambridge, MA: Harvard University Press, 2011.

Wright, Richard. "Between Laughter and Tears." *New Masses* 25 (1937): 22–5.

Young, Kevin. *The Grey Album: On the Blackness of Blackness*. Minneapolis: Graywolf Press, 2012.

THE MACAT LIBRARY
BY DISCIPLINE

AFRICANA STUDIES

Chinua Achebe's *An Image of Africa: Racism in Conrad's Heart of Darkness*
W. E. B. Du Bois's *The Souls of Black Folk*
Zora Neale Huston's *Characteristics of Negro Expression*
Martin Luther King Jr's *Why We Can't Wait*
Toni Morrison's *Playing in the Dark: Whiteness in the American Literary Imagination*

ANTHROPOLOGY

Arjun Appadurai's *Modernity at Large: Cultural Dimensions of Globalisation*
Philippe Ariès's *Centuries of Childhood*
Franz Boas's *Race, Language and Culture*
Kim Chan & Renée Mauborgne's *Blue Ocean Strategy*
Jared Diamond's *Guns, Germs & Steel: the Fate of Human Societies*
Jared Diamond's *Collapse: How Societies Choose to Fail or Survive*
E. E. Evans-Pritchard's *Witchcraft, Oracles and Magic Among the Azande*
James Ferguson's *The Anti-Politics Machine*
Clifford Geertz's *The Interpretation of Cultures*
David Graeber's *Debt: the First 5000 Years*
Karen Ho's *Liquidated: An Ethnography of Wall Street*
Geert Hofstede's *Culture's Consequences: Comparing Values, Behaviors, Institutes and Organizations across Nations*
Claude Lévi-Strauss's *Structural Anthropology*
Jay Macleod's *Ain't No Makin' It: Aspirations and Attainment in a Low-Income Neighborhood*
Saba Mahmood's *The Politics of Piety: The Islamic Revival and the Feminist Subject*
Marcel Mauss's *The Gift*

BUSINESS

Jean Lave & Etienne Wenger's *Situated Learning*
Theodore Levitt's *Marketing Myopia*
Burton G. Malkiel's *A Random Walk Down Wall Street*
Douglas McGregor's *The Human Side of Enterprise*
Michael Porter's *Competitive Strategy: Creating and Sustaining Superior Performance*
John Kotter's *Leading Change*
C. K. Prahalad & Gary Hamel's *The Core Competence of the Corporation*

CRIMINOLOGY

Michelle Alexander's *The New Jim Crow: Mass Incarceration in the Age of Colorblindness*
Michael R. Gottfredson & Travis Hirschi's *A General Theory of Crime*
Richard Herrnstein & Charles A. Murray's *The Bell Curve: Intelligence and Class Structure in American Life*
Elizabeth Loftus's *Eyewitness Testimony*
Jay Macleod's *Ain't No Makin' It: Aspirations and Attainment in a Low-Income Neighborhood*
Philip Zimbardo's *The Lucifer Effect*

ECONOMICS

Janet Abu-Lughod's *Before European Hegemony*
Ha-Joon Chang's *Kicking Away the Ladder*
David Brion Davis's *The Problem of Slavery in the Age of Revolution*
Milton Friedman's *The Role of Monetary Policy*
Milton Friedman's *Capitalism and Freedom*
David Graeber's *Debt: the First 5000 Years*
Friedrich Hayek's *The Road to Serfdom*
Karen Ho's *Liquidated: An Ethnography of Wall Street*

John Maynard Keynes's *The General Theory of Employment, Interest and Money*
Charles P. Kindleberger's *Manias, Panics and Crashes*
Robert Lucas's *Why Doesn't Capital Flow from Rich to Poor Countries?*
Burton G. Malkiel's *A Random Walk Down Wall Street*
Thomas Robert Malthus's *An Essay on the Principle of Population*
Karl Marx's *Capital*
Thomas Piketty's *Capital in the Twenty-First Century*
Amartya Sen's *Development as Freedom*
Adam Smith's *The Wealth of Nations*
Nassim Nicholas Taleb's *The Black Swan: The Impact of the Highly Improbable*
Amos Tversky's & Daniel Kahneman's *Judgment under Uncertainty: Heuristics and Biases*
Mahbub Ul Haq's *Reflections on Human Development*
Max Weber's *The Protestant Ethic and the Spirit of Capitalism*

FEMINISM AND GENDER STUDIES

Judith Butler's *Gender Trouble*
Simone De Beauvoir's *The Second Sex*
Michel Foucault's *History of Sexuality*
Betty Friedan's *The Feminine Mystique*
Saba Mahmood's *The Politics of Piety: The Islamic Revival and the Feminist Subject*
Joan Wallach Scott's *Gender and the Politics of History*
Mary Wollstonecraft's *A Vindication of the Rights of Woman*
Virginia Woolf's *A Room of One's Own*

GEOGRAPHY

The Brundtland Report's *Our Common Future*
Rachel Carson's *Silent Spring*
Charles Darwin's *On the Origin of Species*
James Ferguson's *The Anti-Politics Machine*
Jane Jacobs's *The Death and Life of Great American Cities*
James Lovelock's *Gaia: A New Look at Life on Earth*
Amartya Sen's *Development as Freedom*
Mathis Wackernagel & William Rees's *Our Ecological Footprint*

HISTORY

Janet Abu-Lughod's *Before European Hegemony*
Benedict Anderson's *Imagined Communities*
Bernard Bailyn's *The Ideological Origins of the American Revolution*
Hanna Batatu's *The Old Social Classes And The Revolutionary Movements Of Iraq*
Christopher Browning's *Ordinary Men: Reserve Police Batallion 101 and the Final Solution in Poland*
Edmund Burke's *Reflections on the Revolution in France*
William Cronon's *Nature's Metropolis: Chicago And The Great West*
Alfred W. Crosby's *The Columbian Exchange*
Hamid Dabashi's *Iran: A People Interrupted*
David Brion Davis's *The Problem of Slavery in the Age of Revolution*
Nathalie Zemon Davis's *The Return of Martin Guerre*
Jared Diamond's *Guns, Germs & Steel: the Fate of Human Societies*
Frank Dikotter's *Mao's Great Famine*
John W Dower's *War Without Mercy: Race And Power In The Pacific War*
W. E. B. Du Bois's *The Souls of Black Folk*
Richard J. Evans's *In Defence of History*
Lucien Febvre's *The Problem of Unbelief in the 16th Century*
Sheila Fitzpatrick's *Everyday Stalinism*

Eric Foner's *Reconstruction: America's Unfinished Revolution, 1863-1877*
Michel Foucault's *Discipline and Punish*
Michel Foucault's *History of Sexuality*
Francis Fukuyama's *The End of History and the Last Man*
John Lewis Gaddis's *We Now Know: Rethinking Cold War History*
Ernest Gellner's *Nations and Nationalism*
Eugene Genovese's *Roll, Jordan, Roll: The World the Slaves Made*
Carlo Ginzburg's *The Night Battles*
Daniel Goldhagen's *Hitler's Willing Executioners*
Jack Goldstone's *Revolution and Rebellion in the Early Modern World*
Antonio Gramsci's *The Prison Notebooks*
Alexander Hamilton, John Jay & James Madison's *The Federalist Papers*
Christopher Hill's *The World Turned Upside Down*
Carole Hillenbrand's *The Crusades: Islamic Perspectives*
Thomas Hobbes's *Leviathan*
Eric Hobsbawm's *The Age Of Revolution*
John A. Hobson's *Imperialism: A Study*
Albert Hourani's *History of the Arab Peoples*
Samuel P. Huntington's *The Clash of Civilizations and the Remaking of World Order*
C. L. R. James's *The Black Jacobins*
Tony Judt's *Postwar: A History of Europe Since 1945*
Ernst Kantorowicz's *The King's Two Bodies: A Study in Medieval Political Theology*
Paul Kennedy's *The Rise and Fall of the Great Powers*
Ian Kershaw's *The "Hitler Myth": Image and Reality in the Third Reich*
John Maynard Keynes's *The General Theory of Employment, Interest and Money*
Charles P. Kindleberger's *Manias, Panics and Crashes*
Martin Luther King Jr's *Why We Can't Wait*
Henry Kissinger's *World Order: Reflections on the Character of Nations and the Course of History*
Thomas Kuhn's *The Structure of Scientific Revolutions*
Georges Lefebvre's *The Coming of the French Revolution*
John Locke's *Two Treatises of Government*
Niccolò Machiavelli's *The Prince*
Thomas Robert Malthus's *An Essay on the Principle of Population*
Mahmood Mamdani's *Citizen and Subject: Contemporary Africa And The Legacy Of Late Colonialism*
Karl Marx's *Capital*
Stanley Milgram's *Obedience to Authority*
John Stuart Mill's *On Liberty*
Thomas Paine's *Common Sense*
Thomas Paine's *Rights of Man*
Geoffrey Parker's *Global Crisis: War, Climate Change and Catastrophe in the Seventeenth Century*
Jonathan Riley-Smith's *The First Crusade and the Idea of Crusading*
Jean-Jacques Rousseau's *The Social Contract*
Joan Wallach Scott's *Gender and the Politics of History*
Theda Skocpol's *States and Social Revolutions*
Adam Smith's *The Wealth of Nations*
Timothy Snyder's *Bloodlands: Europe Between Hitler and Stalin*
Sun Tzu's *The Art of War*
Keith Thomas's *Religion and the Decline of Magic*
Thucydides's *The History of the Peloponnesian War*
Frederick Jackson Turner's *The Significance of the Frontier in American History*
Odd Arne Westad's *The Global Cold War: Third World Interventions And The Making Of Our Times*

LITERATURE

Chinua Achebe's *An Image of Africa: Racism in Conrad's Heart of Darkness*
Roland Barthes's *Mythologies*
Homi K. Bhabha's *The Location of Culture*
Judith Butler's *Gender Trouble*
Simone De Beauvoir's *The Second Sex*
Ferdinand De Saussure's *Course in General Linguistics*
T. S. Eliot's *The Sacred Wood: Essays on Poetry and Criticism*
Zora Neale Huston's *Characteristics of Negro Expression*
Toni Morrison's *Playing in the Dark: Whiteness in the American Literary Imagination*
Edward Said's *Orientalism*
Gayatri Chakravorty Spivak's *Can the Subaltern Speak?*
Mary Wollstonecraft's *A Vindication of the Rights of Women*
Virginia Woolf's *A Room of One's Own*

PHILOSOPHY

Elizabeth Anscombe's *Modern Moral Philosophy*
Hannah Arendt's *The Human Condition*
Aristotle's *Metaphysics*
Aristotle's *Nicomachean Ethics*
Edmund Gettier's *Is Justified True Belief Knowledge?*
Georg Wilhelm Friedrich Hegel's *Phenomenology of Spirit*
David Hume's *Dialogues Concerning Natural Religion*
David Hume's *The Enquiry for Human Understanding*
Immanuel Kant's *Religion within the Boundaries of Mere Reason*
Immanuel Kant's *Critique of Pure Reason*
Søren Kierkegaard's *The Sickness Unto Death*
Søren Kierkegaard's *Fear and Trembling*
C. S. Lewis's *The Abolition of Man*
Alasdair MacIntyre's *After Virtue*
Marcus Aurelius's *Meditations*
Friedrich Nietzsche's *On the Genealogy of Morality*
Friedrich Nietzsche's *Beyond Good and Evil*
Plato's *Republic*
Plato's *Symposium*
Jean-Jacques Rousseau's *The Social Contract*
Gilbert Ryle's *The Concept of Mind*
Baruch Spinoza's *Ethics*
Sun Tzu's *The Art of War*
Ludwig Wittgenstein's *Philosophical Investigations*

POLITICS

Benedict Anderson's *Imagined Communities*
Aristotle's *Politics*
Bernard Bailyn's *The Ideological Origins of the American Revolution*
Edmund Burke's *Reflections on the Revolution in France*
John C. Calhoun's *A Disquisition on Government*
Ha-Joon Chang's *Kicking Away the Ladder*
Hamid Dabashi's *Iran: A People Interrupted*
Hamid Dabashi's *Theology of Discontent: The Ideological Foundation of the Islamic Revolution in Iran*
Robert Dahl's *Democracy and its Critics*
Robert Dahl's *Who Governs?*
David Brion Davis's *The Problem of Slavery in the Age of Revolution*

Alexis De Tocqueville's *Democracy in America*
James Ferguson's *The Anti-Politics Machine*
Frank Dikotter's *Mao's Great Famine*
Sheila Fitzpatrick's *Everyday Stalinism*
Eric Foner's *Reconstruction: America's Unfinished Revolution, 1863-1877*
Milton Friedman's *Capitalism and Freedom*
Francis Fukuyama's *The End of History and the Last Man*
John Lewis Gaddis's *We Now Know: Rethinking Cold War History*
Ernest Gellner's *Nations and Nationalism*
David Graeber's *Debt: the First 5000 Years*
Antonio Gramsci's *The Prison Notebooks*
Alexander Hamilton, John Jay & James Madison's *The Federalist Papers*
Friedrich Hayek's *The Road to Serfdom*
Christopher Hill's *The World Turned Upside Down*
Thomas Hobbes's *Leviathan*
John A. Hobson's *Imperialism: A Study*
Samuel P. Huntington's *The Clash of Civilizations and the Remaking of World Order*
Tony Judt's *Postwar: A History of Europe Since 1945*
David C. Kang's *China Rising: Peace, Power and Order in East Asia*
Paul Kennedy's *The Rise and Fall of Great Powers*
Robert Keohane's *After Hegemony*
Martin Luther King Jr.'s *Why We Can't Wait*
Henry Kissinger's *World Order: Reflections on the Character of Nations and the Course of History*
John Locke's *Two Treatises of Government*
Niccolò Machiavelli's *The Prince*
Thomas Robert Malthus's *An Essay on the Principle of Population*
Mahmood Mamdani's *Citizen and Subject: Contemporary Africa And The Legacy Of Late Colonialism*
Karl Marx's *Capital*
John Stuart Mill's *On Liberty*
John Stuart Mill's *Utilitarianism*
Hans Morgenthau's *Politics Among Nations*
Thomas Paine's *Common Sense*
Thomas Paine's *Rights of Man*
Thomas Piketty's *Capital in the Twenty-First Century*
Robert D. Putman's *Bowling Alone*
John Rawls's *Theory of Justice*
Jean-Jacques Rousseau's *The Social Contract*
Theda Skocpol's *States and Social Revolutions*
Adam Smith's *The Wealth of Nations*
Sun Tzu's *The Art of War*
Henry David Thoreau's *Civil Disobedience*
Thucydides's *The History of the Peloponnesian War*
Kenneth Waltz's *Theory of International Politics*
Max Weber's *Politics as a Vocation*
Odd Arne Westad's *The Global Cold War: Third World Interventions And The Making Of Our Times*

POSTCOLONIAL STUDIES

Roland Barthes's *Mythologies*
Frantz Fanon's *Black Skin, White Masks*
Homi K. Bhabha's *The Location of Culture*
Gustavo Gutiérrez's *A Theology of Liberation*
Edward Said's *Orientalism*
Gayatri Chakravorty Spivak's *Can the Subaltern Speak?*

PSYCHOLOGY

Gordon Allport's *The Nature of Prejudice*
Alan Baddeley & Graham Hitch's *Aggression: A Social Learning Analysis*
Albert Bandura's *Aggression: A Social Learning Analysis*
Leon Festinger's *A Theory of Cognitive Dissonance*
Sigmund Freud's *The Interpretation of Dreams*
Betty Friedan's *The Feminine Mystique*
Michael R. Gottfredson & Travis Hirschi's *A General Theory of Crime*
Eric Hoffer's *The True Believer: Thoughts on the Nature of Mass Movements*
William James's *Principles of Psychology*
Elizabeth Loftus's *Eyewitness Testimony*
A. H. Maslow's *A Theory of Human Motivation*
Stanley Milgram's *Obedience to Authority*
Steven Pinker's *The Better Angels of Our Nature*
Oliver Sacks's *The Man Who Mistook His Wife For a Hat*
Richard Thaler & Cass Sunstein's *Nudge: Improving Decisions About Health, Wealth and Happiness*
Amos Tversky's *Judgment under Uncertainty: Heuristics and Biases*
Philip Zimbardo's *The Lucifer Effect*

SCIENCE

Rachel Carson's *Silent Spring*
William Cronon's *Nature's Metropolis: Chicago And The Great West*
Alfred W. Crosby's *The Columbian Exchange*
Charles Darwin's *On the Origin of Species*
Richard Dawkin's *The Selfish Gene*
Thomas Kuhn's *The Structure of Scientific Revolutions*
Geoffrey Parker's *Global Crisis: War, Climate Change and Catastrophe in the Seventeenth Century*
Mathis Wackernagel & William Rees's *Our Ecological Footprint*

SOCIOLOGY

Michelle Alexander's *The New Jim Crow: Mass Incarceration in the Age of Colorblindness*
Gordon Allport's *The Nature of Prejudice*
Albert Bandura's *Aggression: A Social Learning Analysis*
Hanna Batatu's *The Old Social Classes And The Revolutionary Movements Of Iraq*
Ha-Joon Chang's *Kicking Away the Ladder*
W. E. B. Du Bois's *The Souls of Black Folk*
Émile Durkheim's *On Suicide*
Frantz Fanon's *Black Skin, White Masks*
Frantz Fanon's *The Wretched of the Earth*
Eric Foner's *Reconstruction: America's Unfinished Revolution, 1863-1877*
Eugene Genovese's *Roll, Jordan, Roll: The World the Slaves Made*
Jack Goldstone's *Revolution and Rebellion in the Early Modern World*
Antonio Gramsci's *The Prison Notebooks*
Richard Herrnstein & Charles A Murray's *The Bell Curve: Intelligence and Class Structure in American Life*
Eric Hoffer's *The True Believer: Thoughts on the Nature of Mass Movements*
Jane Jacobs's *The Death and Life of Great American Cities*
Robert Lucas's *Why Doesn't Capital Flow from Rich to Poor Countries?*
Jay Macleod's *Ain't No Makin' It: Aspirations and Attainment in a Low Income Neighborhood*
Elaine May's *Homeward Bound: American Families in the Cold War Era*
Douglas McGregor's *The Human Side of Enterprise*
C. Wright Mills's *The Sociological Imagination*

Thomas Piketty's *Capital in the Twenty-First Century*
Robert D. Putman's *Bowling Alone*
David Riesman's *The Lonely Crowd: A Study of the Changing American Character*
Edward Said's *Orientalism*
Joan Wallach Scott's *Gender and the Politics of History*
Theda Skocpol's *States and Social Revolutions*
Max Weber's *The Protestant Ethic and the Spirit of Capitalism*

THEOLOGY

Augustine's *Confessions*
Benedict's *Rule of St Benedict*
Gustavo Gutiérrez's *A Theology of Liberation*
Carole Hillenbrand's *The Crusades: Islamic Perspectives*
David Hume's *Dialogues Concerning Natural Religion*
Immanuel Kant's *Religion within the Boundaries of Mere Reason*
Ernst Kantorowicz's *The King's Two Bodies: A Study in Medieval Political Theology*
Søren Kierkegaard's *The Sickness Unto Death*
C. S. Lewis's *The Abolition of Man*
Saba Mahmood's *The Politics of Piety: The Islamic Revival and the Feminist Subject*
Baruch Spinoza's *Ethics*
Keith Thomas's *Religion and the Decline of Magic*

COMING SOON

Chris Argyris's *The Individual and the Organisation*
Seyla Benhabib's *The Rights of Others*
Walter Benjamin's *The Work Of Art in the Age of Mechanical Reproduction*
John Berger's *Ways of Seeing*
Pierre Bourdieu's *Outline of a Theory of Practice*
Mary Douglas's *Purity and Danger*
Roland Dworkin's *Taking Rights Seriously*
James G. March's *Exploration and Exploitation in Organisational Learning*
Ikujiro Nonaka's *A Dynamic Theory of Organizational Knowledge Creation*
Griselda Pollock's *Vision and Difference*
Amartya Sen's *Inequality Re-Examined*
Susan Sontag's *On Photography*
Yasser Tabbaa's *The Transformation of Islamic Art*
Ludwig von Mises's *Theory of Money and Credit*

Macat Disciplines

Access the greatest ideas and thinkers across entire disciplines, including

Postcolonial Studies

Roland Barthes's *Mythologies*
Frantz Fanon's *Black Skin, White Masks*
Homi K. Bhabha's *The Location of Culture*
Gustavo Gutiérrez's *A Theology of Liberation*
Edward Said's *Orientalism*
Gayatri Chakravorty Spivak's *Can the Subaltern Speak?*

Macat Disciplines

Access the greatest ideas and thinkers across entire disciplines, including

AFRICANA STUDIES

Chinua Achebe's *An Image of Africa: Racism in Conrad's Heart of Darkness*

W. E. B. Du Bois's *The Souls of Black Folk*

Zora Neale Hurston's *Characteristics of Negro Expression*

Martin Luther King Jr.'s *Why We Can't Wait*

Toni Morrison's *Playing in the Dark: Whiteness in the American Literary Imagination*

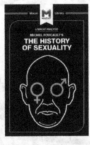

Macat Disciplines

*Access the greatest ideas and thinkers
across entire disciplines, including*

CRIMINOLOGY

Michelle Alexander's
*The New Jim Crow:
Mass Incarceration in the
Age of Colorblindness*

**Michael R. Gottfredson
& Travis Hirschi's**
A General Theory of Crime

Elizabeth Loftus's
Eyewitness Testimony

**Richard Herrnstein
& Charles A. Murray's**
*The Bell Curve: Intelligence and
Class Structure in American Life*

Jay Macleod's
*Ain't No Makin' It:
Aspirations and Attainment in a
Low-Income Neighborhood*

Philip Zimbardo's
The Lucifer Effect

Macat Disciplines

*Access the greatest ideas and thinkers
across entire disciplines, including*

INEQUALITY

Ha-Joon Chang's, *Kicking Away the Ladder*

David Graeber's, *Debt: The First 5000 Years*

Robert E. Lucas's, *Why Doesn't Capital Flow from
Rich To Poor Countries?*

Thomas Piketty's, *Capital in the Twenty-First Century*

Amartya Sen's, *Inequality Re-Examined*

Mahbub Ul Haq's, *Reflections on Human Development*

Macat analyses are available from all good bookshops and libraries.

Access hundreds of analyses through one, multimedia tool.
Join free for one month **library.macat.com**

Macat Disciplines

Access the greatest ideas and thinkers across entire disciplines, including

MAN AND THE ENVIRONMENT

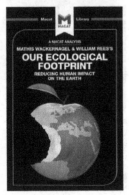

The Brundtland Report's, *Our Common Future*

Rachel Carson's, *Silent Spring*

James Lovelock's, *Gaia: A New Look at Life on Earth*

Mathis Wackernagel & William Rees's, *Our Ecological Footprint*

Macat analyses are available from all good bookshops and libraries.

Access hundreds of analyses through one, multimedia tool.
Join free for one month **library.macat.com**

Macat Disciplines

Access the greatest ideas and thinkers across entire disciplines, including

THE FUTURE OF DEMOCRACY

Robert A. Dahl's, *Democracy and Its Critics*
Robert A. Dahl's, *Who Governs?*
Alexis De Toqueville's, *Democracy in America*
Niccolò Machiavelli's, *The Prince*
John Stuart Mill's, *On Liberty*
Robert D. Putnam's, *Bowling Alone*
Jean-Jacques Rousseau's, *The Social Contract*
Henry David Thoreau's, *Civil Disobedience*

Macat Disciplines

Access the greatest ideas and thinkers across entire disciplines, including

TOTALITARIANISM

Sheila Fitzpatrick's, *Everyday Stalinism*
Ian Kershaw's, *The "Hitler Myth"*
Timothy Snyder's, *Bloodlands*

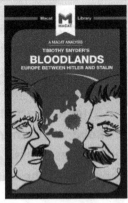

Macat Pairs

Analyse historical and modern issues from opposite sides of an argument. Pairs include:

RACE AND IDENTITY

Zora Neale Hurston's
Characteristics of Negro Expression

Using material collected on anthropological expeditions to the South, Zora Neale Hurston explains how expression in African American culture in the early twentieth century departs from the art of white America. At the time, African American art was often criticized for copying white culture. For Hurston, this criticism misunderstood how art works. European tradition views art as something fixed. But Hurston describes a creative process that is alive, ever-changing, and largely improvisational. She maintains that African American art works through a process called 'mimicry'—where an imitated object or verbal pattern, for example, is reshaped and altered until it becomes something new, novel—and worthy of attention.

Frantz Fanon's
Black Skin, White Masks

Black Skin, White Masks offers a radical analysis of the psychological effects of colonization on the colonized.

Fanon witnessed the effects of colonization first hand both in his birthplace, Martinique, and again later in life when he worked as a psychiatrist in another French colony, Algeria. His text is uncompromising in form and argument. He dissects the dehumanizing effects of colonialism, arguing that it destroys the native sense of identity, forcing people to adapt to an alien set of values—including a core belief that they are inferior. This results in deep psychological trauma.

Fanon's work played a pivotal role in the civil rights movements of the 1960s.

Macat analyses are available from all good bookshops and libraries.

Access hundreds of analyses through one, multimedia tool.
Join free for one month **library.macat.com**

Macat Pairs

Analyse historical and modern issues from opposite sides of an argument. Pairs include:

INTERNATIONAL RELATIONS IN THE 21ST CENTURY

Samuel P. Huntington's
The Clash of Civilisations
In his highly influential 1996 book, Huntington offers a vision of a post-Cold War world in which conflict takes place not between competing ideologies but between cultures. The worst clash, he argues, will be between the Islamic world and the West: the West's arrogance and belief that its culture is a "gift" to the world will come into conflict with Islam's obstinacy and concern that its culture is under attack from a morally decadent "other."

Clash inspired much debate between different political schools of thought. But its greatest impact came in helping define American foreign policy in the wake of the 2001 terrorist attacks in New York and Washington.

Francis Fukuyama's
The End of History and the Last Man
Published in 1992, *The End of History and the Last Man* argues that capitalist democracy is the final destination for all societies. Fukuyama believed democracy triumphed during the Cold War because it lacks the "fundamental contradictions" inherent in communism and satisfies our yearning for freedom and equality. Democracy therefore marks the endpoint in the evolution of ideology, and so the "end of history." There will still be "events," but no fundamental change in ideology.

Macat analyses are available from all good bookshops and libraries.

Access hundreds of analyses through one, multimedia tool.
Join free for one month **library.macat.com**

Macat Pairs

Analyse historical and modern issues from opposite sides of an argument. Pairs include:

ARE WE FUNDAMENTALLY GOOD - OR BAD?

Steven Pinker's
The Better Angels of Our Nature

Stephen Pinker's gloriously optimistic 2011 book argues that, despite humanity's biological tendency toward violence, we are, in fact, less violent today than ever before. To prove his case, Pinker lays out pages of detailed statistical evidence. For him, much of the credit for the decline goes to the eighteenth-century Enlightenment movement, whose ideas of liberty, tolerance, and respect for the value of human life filtered down through society and affected how people thought. That psychological change led to behavioral change—and overall we became more peaceful. Critics countered that humanity could never overcome the biological urge toward violence; others argued that Pinker's statistics were flawed.

Philip Zimbardo's
The Lucifer Effect

Some psychologists believe those who commit cruelty are innately evil. Zimbardo disagrees. In *The Lucifer Effect*, he argues that sometimes good people do evil things simply because of the situations they find themselves in, citing many historical examples to illustrate his point. Zimbardo details his 1971 Stanford prison experiment, where ordinary volunteers playing guards in a mock prison rapidly became abusive. But he also describes the tortures committed by US army personnel in Iraq's Abu Ghraib prison in 2003—and how he himself testified in defence of one of those guards. committed by US army personnel in Iraq's Abu Ghraib prison in 2003—and how he himself testified in defence of one of those guards.

Macat analyses are available from all good bookshops and libraries.

Access hundreds of analyses through one, multimedia tool.
Join free for one month **library.macat.com**

Macat Pairs

Analyse historical and modern issues from opposite sides of an argument. Pairs include:

HOW WE RELATE TO EACH OTHER AND SOCIETY

Jean-Jacques Rousseau's
The Social Contract

Rousseau's famous work sets out the radical concept of the 'social contract': a give-and-take relationship between individual freedom and social order.

If people are free to do as they like, governed only by their own sense of justice, they are also vulnerable to chaos and violence. To avoid this, Rousseau proposes, they should agree to give up some freedom to benefit from the protection of social and political organization. But this deal is only just if societies are led by the collective needs and desires of the people, and able to control the private interests of individuals. For Rousseau, the only legitimate form of government is rule by the people.

Robert D. Putnam's
Bowling Alone

In *Bowling Alone*, Robert Putnam argues that Americans have become disconnected from one another and from the institutions of their common life, and investigates the consequences of this change.

Looking at a range of indicators, from membership in formal organizations to the number of invitations being extended to informal dinner parties, Putnam demonstrates that Americans are interacting less and creating less "social capital" – with potentially disastrous implications for their society.

It would be difficult to overstate the impact of *Bowling Alone*, one of the most frequently cited social science publications of the last half-century.

Macat analyses are available from all good bookshops and libraries.

Access hundreds of analyses through one, multimedia tool.
Join free for one month **library.macat.com**

Printed in the United States
by Baker & Taylor Publisher Services